WHAT IS LOVE
Awakening the Truth for Healthy Relationships

BJ O'NEAL, JR.

Copyright © 2018 by BJ O'Neal, Jr.

All rights reserved. No part of this book may be reproduced or transmitted in any form or by any means, electronic or mechanical, including photocopying, recording or by any information storage and retrieval system, without the permission in writing from the copyright owner.

ISBN: 978-1-9857-0506-7

This book was printed in the United States of America.

Scripture quotations taken from the Amplified Bible (AMP), Copyright © 2015 by The Lockman Foundation Used by permission. www.Lockman.org

CONTENTS

What is Love? 5
Love is Patient 11
Love is Kind 18
Love Does Not Envy 27
It Does Not Boast 34
It is Not Proud 41
It is not Rude 49
It is not Self-Seeking 61
It is not Easily Angered 74
It Keeps No Record of Wrongs 87
Love Does Not Delight in Evil but
Rejoices with the Truth 101
Love Always Protects 115
Love Always Trusts 132
Love Always Hopes 142
Love Always Perseveres 154
Love Never Fails 168

DEDICATION:

To my beautiful wife, Stephanie, for being so incredible and the reason I strive to understand and operate in authentic love.

To Naomi, Benjamin and Tylaseua for being my motivation to be a better example.

INTRODUCTION:
What is Love?

"If I speak with the tongues of men and of angels, but have not love [for others growing out of God's love for me], then I become only on a noisy gong or a clanging cymbal [just an annoying distraction]. And I have the gift of prophecy [and speak a new message from God to the people], and understand all mysteries, and [possess] all knowledge; and if I have all [sufficient] faith so that I can remove mountains, but do not have love [reaching out to others], I am nothing. If I give all of my possessions to feed the poor, and if I surrender my body to be burned, but not have love, it does me no good at all." ~ I Cor. 13:1-3 AMP

Don't mistakenly believe that love is not relevant in today's time. It is very vital. In fact, it is clear that,

WHAT IS LOVE

without knowing how to and demonstrating love, we are useless, even in the things we are gifted to do. Even our sacrifices are worthless. Love is necessary.

In the Bible, someone following Jesus asked Him what was the most important commandment in the law, and Jesus replied. The conversation went like this:

> *"Teacher, which is the greatest commandment in the Law?' And Jesus replied to him, 'You shall love the Lord with all your heart, and with all your soul, and with all your mind. This is the first and greatest commandment. The second is like it, You shall love your neighbor as yourself [that is, unselfishly seek the best or higher good for others]. The whole Law and [the writing of the] Prophets depend on these commandments.'"*
> *~ Matthew 22:36-40 AMP*

In pure love, you'd fully fulfill your commitments to one another.

You could not fulfill God's commandments apart from love. In pure love, you could fulfill them all. Likewise, love is vital to fruitful, successful relationships and marriages. In pure love, you'd fully fulfill your commitments to one another. Indeed, your relationship will be fruitful and successful with love, but it cannot be without it.

A major problem that exists in today's time is that we lack the proper reverence for love, therefore we mildly if not only conveniently apply it. The other major problem is that we don't fully understand love or how to love so we fail to operate in it, so most of our efforts become fruitless or bare bad fruit. This was my wife and I at the beginning of our marriage. We were excited and in love on the wedding day. However, shortly afterwards, there was so much disappointment because we felt the other person was not keeping with our expectations and we felt unappreciated in what we felt we were bringing to the table. It was an equation for disaster.

Now, I imagine a large percent of wedding ceremonies include the reading of the scripture, I Corinthians 13: "Love is patient, love is kind, love is..." It sounds beautiful and everyone present is just elated to see the two people unite. However, I believe, rarely ever are the words reflected on at that time and possibly no time after that. They leave no impression on the heart, just a faint memory of something that happened during the wedding ceremony. I, honestly, can't remember whether or not it was read at our wedding. I think it was, but I'm not certain.

I believe that is a mistake (not the scripture that was chosen, but the failure to take in what was said). Unfortunately, I believe the scripture has become so cliché that it has lost its power and application due to how it is popularly used.

However, we will journey together in these pages to break down every part of how love is defined in I Corinthians 13 and other scriptures. In preparing this material, a friend voiced how a speaker at a marriage conference pointed out that Paul was not actually talking about marriage in these scriptures, and I have no reason to disagree with the speaker. The speaker mentioned that, when Paul talked about marriage, he instructed husbands to "love your wives as Christ loved the church." This is great instruction for husbands, but, again, what does that love look like? I

WHAT IS LOVE

Corinthians 13 takes its time to define what love is and what love isn't. To love like Christ, we must understand love. The more we understand love, the more we understand God.

"Beloved, let us [unselfishly] love and seek the best for one another, for love is from God, and everyone who loves [others] is born of God and knows God [through personal experience]. The one who does not love has not become acquainted with God [does not and never did know him], for God is love. [He is the originator of love, and it is an enduring attribute of his nature]." ~ I John 4:7-8

How well you know love is a testament of how well you know God. That's profound! It also says that you don't even know God if you are not actively loving. Ouch! Again, the scripture reveals how empty and void we are without love. According to these scriptures, how can we expect to effectively walk with God without understanding and operating in love? God built and covenanted his relationship with us through love. Do we really expect our relationships to thrive through other means? We cannot expect to implore worldly ways through worldly vises and expect things that are spiritual to flourish.

A year into our marriage, we had already beaten each other up with our imperfect views and flaws. To top it off, neither one of us was seeking help. We sought fulfillment. We were so ugly to each other. We were pulling apart very early on. Unhappy, self-righteous and selfish, I violated the purity that remained in our marriage. We were facing a divorce. Though the divorce did not come, full reconciliation hadn't manifested. It has been a great journey working to heal wounds and operate in healthy matrimony. Through the journey, I had grown quite a bit, but I felt like I personally hit a plateau, though I know hadn't "arrived."

In the past, I've flawed on so many occasions attempting to love through the perversions I had come to identify love with, and I have felt the weight and the burn of those errors. As a husband and a father, I realized I needed to humble myself, prepare to cast away any part of me that inhibits my ability to love the way God has commissioned me to do. I have made it my mission and desire to settle for nothing less than full reconciliation. I want to love my wife the way God intended for me to love her in the first place. Five years into recovery, still not where I believed we should've been, I made it my deepest desire to further call on God to help me better understand what it means to love someone. Love transcends into every aspect of life and we all share a responsibility in it. I hope you, too, are willing to humble yourself, place yourself as clay, ready and willing to be shaped in the purpose God has intended for you to live out in your relationships. What is love? Allow the truth to be awakened in you, that you may fulfill love's calling in your relationships.

What is the Meaning?

What is love's meaning? I've been dreaming of being immersed in bliss, yet I miss every opportunity to do so. I'm screaming. I spent too much time leaning on my own understanding, demanding her to do the same. Desire wanting her to stay. Pride willing to let her go. Nothing left to show for love but a grudge because things never seem to work out with good intentions.

WHAT IS LOVE

I thought I was being a good man, can't understand how my plans failed and our problems prevailed. Do I try it again? So much apprehension!
But I can't give up. I need to find a way to live up to love's expectations.
I can't expect her to just put up with what drives her away. Come back to me! I'll change to make ecstasy our destination.
Recalculating... make a U-turn, this hurt burns so much I wish we'd never have to experience it again.
Learning to stay in my lane. God, send me the signals to steer through the pain. Guide our hearts to the promised land.
Teach me how to love. Remind me that she's enough to bear my own cross to cross the threshold into a greater truth.
Divine wisdom, breaking down the light through a prism, restoring the innocence and faith of our youth.
Love is waiting for us. We must chase towards it with courage and hope,
That it's as righteous as it sounds, that we will experience peace once it surrounds our hearts, fashioning the cord of three - the unbreakable rope.

CHAPTER 1:
Love is Patient

Patient - bearing provocation, annoyance, misfortune, delay, hardship, pain, etc., with fortitude and calm without complaint, anger or the like. Quietly and steadily persevering or diligent, especially in detail and exactness.

From the definition, I'd like to pull out some deductive reasoning:

- You cannot operate in actual patience without the presence of some form of discomfort or agitation.
- Patience has more to do with your character and actions in the presence of these ongoing discomforts and agitations.

- The level of patience demonstrated increases with the manner of character and conduct exemplified considering the level of annoyance and length of time under such annoyance. This means the more fortitude and calmness you operate in the presence of a great pain over a great length of time indicates that you would operate with a high level of patience.
- Patience is not the ability to wait but how you operate while waiting. And I actually want to site a scripture to back it up:

"But the fruit of the Spirit [the result of His presence in us] is love [unselfish concern for others], joy, [inner] peace, patience [not the ability to wait, but how we act while waiting]..."
~ Galatians 5:22 AMP

In this verse, we also see that patience is a spiritual fruit that is gained as God dwells inside of us. Patience grows and matures us, making us better use to God, others and ourselves.

And not only this, but [with joy] let us exalt (to show or feel a lively or triumphant joy) in our sufferings and rejoice in our hardships, knowing that our hardship (distress, pressure, trouble) produces patient endurance; and endurance, proven character (spiritual maturity); and proven character, hope and confident assurance [of eternal salvation]. ~ Romans 5:3-4

Patience rejoices in our suffering over time, yet in our relationships we tend to complain and grow weary over time. In these moments our character fails. Triumphant joy! Patience reminds you constantly that you will be triumphant over the hardships. Our endurance will do a good work in us if we allow it! We tend to run from or become discouraged in our hardships that we experience in our relationships. We form resentment towards our mates, accompanied with anger and frustration. However, notice how far down hope was in the series presented in Romans. We never get to hope because we don't allow the hardship to shape our character. So without hope, we give up on our relationships. Even if we don't leave, when we don't see it getting any better and stop looking for it to get better, we give up in our hearts.

> **Patience endures with expectancy.**

Patience asks us "What are we doing while we wait?" Chances are, the reason we get tapped out while waiting is because we stop operating in triumphant joy. I used to have road rage while driving in Houston, TX. When people drove slow, changed lanes unexpectedly, sped by recklessly, and/or due to the numerous areas where traffic was bumper to bumper, anytime of the day, any day of the week, I would be angry, frustrated and enraged. I didn't always express it greatly on the outside, but I felt it greatly on the inside. One day I made the decision that these feelings and reactions were too unhealthy for me. I had to find a way to make peace with the traffic. Otherwise, one day, I would die angry and upset and the traffic would remain. Here are a few things that I realized:

- No matter how bad the traffic is, I get to my destination.

- I cannot control or even confront every single driver on the road, but I can confront and control my own attitude, every time, if I choose.
- If I find ways to enjoy the journey, the traffic is no longer a challenge or burden but an opportunity.

I decided to enjoy my music, sing concerts only I wanted to be a part of, reflect, or plan out choices and decisions I needed to make. I would converse with people that were in the vehicle with me and work to enjoy the conversation. Sometimes, considering the busy schedule I would typically have, I would enjoy a moment to do absolutely nothing.

Have you made up in your mind that no matter how bad the traffic is in your relationship (bad communication, finances, intimacy, hurt, lack of wisdom) that you will still ultimately get to your destination? Have you figured out that you will die trying to control every issue you will ever have with your mate, but you will live as you confront your own issues and improve on your own character? Do you realize that you don't have to wait till the traffic (hardships) is over in your relationship to enjoy yourself and your mate? You may be "stuck in traffic" but sing praises, anyway. Enjoy each other in the moment. You may not be able to do some things, but while you are in hardship, it is an important time to build positive experiences.

"So Jacob served seven years to get Rachel, but they seemed like only a few days to him because of his love for her." ~ Genesis 29:20

Jacob had patience, and Jacob's seven years felt like a few days for a few reasons:

- That is the power of love in effect. If you allow love to permeate through your being, it will give you the strength and courage to endure.
- He had patience because he believed the promise that, in due time, he'd have the woman he loved.
- Lastly, he didn't sit around and simply wait. He kept busy and was productive as he worked to fulfill his part of the deal. Likewise, I believe the time would "fly by" if we focused more on what we can be doing and not on those things we are waiting to change or get better. You may be familiar with the saying, "you can't watch a pot of water boil."

Patience endures with expectancy. I am not suffering for the sake of just suffering! Triumphant joy! We will be triumphant in due time! Where are the Jacobs of today? We need to adopt the Jacob mindset. "He carried two hundred pounds on his shoulders, but it felt like ten because he loved her so much." "She yelled and disrespected him throughout the argument, but he drew her closer and listened because he loved her so much." "She withheld her body from him out of spite and hurt, but he found a thousand other ways to connect with her, in the meantime, because he loved her so much." "He remained disconnected and detached for five years but she wrote songs and poems to express how she felt about him because she knew one day his eyes and ears would be opened, and he'd gladly hear all that she'd been trying to share over those years." Where are we personally inserting our "because I love him/her so much" into our relationships - something that would seem like too much for too long to bear, but love seems to drastically reduce what that endured time feels like?

It has been a long journey to recover the brokenness in our marriage. The reality is that my wife and I travel at two different speeds, concerning reconciliation. Just because I am ready in one area, doesn't mean that she will automatically be ready. In those areas, I am not focused on her not being ready; I'm working in the areas I am ready and aware to work. I continue to work in expectation of her being ready one day. I don't sit back and count the days. Because I don't, I rarely ever have anxiety. Anxiety only arises when I consider the time. If I consider my task and desires, I am determined and fulfilled in displaying my love for her. In this journey, a lot of milestones have came about supernaturally, beyond my control. I have the opportunity to thank God and appreciate her for them.

Love is patient. Unfortunately, because we lack patience, too often, we give up on our relationships prematurely. When the discussions aren't working, when the first few plans fail, we start operating with a defeated mindset. The problems that we are facing ultimately aren't the major problem; it is our flawed character. It is our flawed hearts.

Do you know what happened to Jacob after working seven years to receive Rachel? Laban, her father, gave Jacob his oldest daughter, Leah, instead. He had to marry Leah and give her a week of celebration. He also had to work for Laban for seven more years. Jacob kept his character intact. He honored the man that betrayed the agreement and endured a total of fourteen years of labor all because he had patient love for Rachel. There was no amount of time, no level of labor, that was going to keep him from the love of his life. Patience comes with the right perspective over the situation: "because I love her so much, she is worth the wait."

Worth It

Things don't always happen at the time you want or the way you want, but I won't ever lose sight of my mission. You and me, together forever, in intimate bliss. This will always be my goal. Loving you will always be my decision.
Time will try to convince me that things will never change, so I just rearrange my priorities.
Instead of waiting, I'm participating in the solution, making contributions to the answer. Life will not get the chance to question my loyalty.
Problems will pay high lawyer fees to try me. We will experience victory at the end of the verdict.
Allowing love to persevere and endure, no matter how painful never question it, you're worth it. These trials are working a great purpose in our lives, and I'm willing to allow them to serve it.
Though we'll never be perfect, there is a great treasure in us and patience wants to unearth it and lift it up for world to see.
There is something special between you and me. Time will prove to be the only casualty as we learn to love each other through eternity.

CHAPTER 2:
Love is Kind

Do not let mercy and kindness and truth leave you [instead let these qualities define you]. ~ Proverbs 3:3

Kind - of good or benevolent nature or disposition, indulgent, considerate or helpful

"Let these qualities define you." A profound command from wisdom. We may operate in kindness every now and then, but does it define us? Most of us aren't familiar with this definition of kindness. We have equated being kind to simply being nice to people. Here we find that kindness is a state being where we desire to help or be considerate of another person. In effect, you are placing value and importance on another person's feelings, circumstances, desires, etc.

Here are some examples:

How do I respond to her "daddy issues?"
- I choose my words carefully. I understand her void and hurt, so I make sure my words do not cut away at whatever esteem may exist.
- I filter through her words. I understand that she may often speak out of hurt and abandonment, so I do not take things personally.
- I validate her more - the things she does, her beauty. I support her goals and offer her the encouragement she may not have received from her father.

These are acts of kindness.

In the same likeness, kindness will guide us to how we respond to them being overweight, how we respond to them losing a job, how we respond if she is struggling to get pregnant, and/or how we respond if he used to abuse drugs. Kindness develops us in all of these situations.

> **Kindness sees a need an meets it.**

And the natives showed us extraordinary kindness and hospitality; for they kindled a fire and welcomed us all, since it had begun to rain and was cold. ~ Acts 28:2

  Kindness sees a need and meets it. In fact, a "nice" act is not a kind one without a need in mind that is being met. This is where a common frustration happens in dating, courting and even in marriage. We get disappointed when "nice" acts do not yield the fruit of kind ones. What's the difference? You offer someone a bottle of water... that's nice. Let's establish a setting. You notice they are sweating profusely. They have been doing hard work and are probably approaching dehydration. As compared to a visitor dropping by and hospitably offering a drink to them, there is a distinct connection being made in the first example.

And don't get discouraged, being nice has an important place in relationships of all sorts. Again, we just do not want to blend the two and assume that we are being kind when we are in fact just being nice. In a sense, kindness is nice or thoughtful actions that address a specific need or concern. For example, I can compliment my wife every day. And I'd hope she would appreciate the words of affirmation. I'm sure those words would in fact allow her to know how I view her. However, without a setting, without a perceived need, how intentional can those words be? Now, if she struggled with seeing her beauty, or if she was self-conscious about gaining weight, those words have greater meaning. In fact, if I witnessed her staring in the mirror, and I observed her looking at herself with obvious criticism of her appearance, I'd have the opportunity to kindly remind her of how beautiful she is.

If my mate struggles with low self-esteem, I don't belittle her for it, I offer continuous affirmation. I remind her of what I see in her. If he's been laboring at work or around the house, or is just stressed over circumstances, offer him a massage to relieve his stress. If he/she is desiring to go into business, find them a book or a workshop related to the field of his/her interest. Place value on these things and respond by meeting the needs involved.

I do not want to discourage nice acts; I want us to be aware of the difference and excel at both in our relationships and overall interactions with humanity.

Now, some may not be aware, but love actually has a weapon for when you are being mistreated, when you are being offended, when the person you are with is not "acting right." What do you do when your mate is disappointing you, making you upset or offending you? How to get them to desire the things that draw you closer? How to get them to desire to refrain from doing things that are damaging and draw you away from each other? Believe it or not, kindness is the key.

If your enemy is hungry, give him food to eat; if he is thirsty, give him water to drink. In doing this, you will heap burning coals [of shame] on his head, and the Lord will reward you. - Proverbs 25:21-22; Romans 12:20-21

As we repay our enemies with kindness, likewise, while your mate has offended you, in moments of distress or need, continue to meet the need, not resentfully but in loving kindness. Like the enemy resenting being so foolish to be on the enemy side of someone so compassionate and selfless to meet a real need, so will your mates soon desire to reconcile than to misuse genuine love. Like before, I do want to stress that being nice isn't the same as being kind. Just as before, the example demonstrates being kind as meeting a need. The scripture didn't say simply feed them and give them something to drink. It said, "If they are hungry... if they are thirsty." The power of kindness is that it considers and meets the need.

You've argued about sharing house chores? Clean the house in areas of their concern and allow them to appreciate their concerns being met in that area. Husbands, your wives aren't being intimate? Find a great need they are experiencing, meet it liberally without extending the expectation of sex. Remind them of the joy you get in meeting their needs. Has your mate been verbally abusive? When their actions would naturally make them feel less than, take those moments to verbally affirm them and remind them of their great qualities.

I know what some of you are thinking: "They don't deserve it. I'm not going to be misused, walked on or played the fool." The beauty of it is that you are not playing the fool but operating with the wisdom that these are actually the best opportunities for love to operate in the hearts of those we care about.

At one time we too were foolish, disobedient, deceived and enslaved by all kinds of passions and pleasures. We lived in malice and envy, being hated and hating one another. But when the kindness and love of God our Savior appeared, he saved us, not because of righteous things we have done, but because of his mercy. He saved us through the washing of rebirth and renewal by the Holy Spirit..."
~Titus 3:3-5

The thing I want to point out in this scripture is that God's love and kindness did not show up because we deserved it. Yet, some kind of way, we overlook God's example and place the demand that the people we say we love have to deserve our love and kindness as well. We obviously have no authority above God, but I believe that it is the stubbornness and selfishness of our flesh that places this stipulation into our relationships, but look at God's example.

God was not concerned about being the fool. In fact, he knew our wrong ways was an indication of our own foolishness, yet he was kind and loving anyway. Every Christian has their "salvation story." Some may have come to God in fear of damnation, but I love the fact that mine is filled with overwhelming gratitude and appreciation of the sacrifice God made, despite all of the mistakes I would make, just so that He and I could have a relationship. He truly loves me. Why is it so hard to transfer that love to those we say we love, too?

My wife and I destroyed so much of our relationship, early on by responding negatively to disappointment. We felt we needed to protect ourselves and let it be known that we weren't going to be used or fully committed if we were going to be mistreated or dissatisfied. Let me just say that that was a recipe for disaster. It led to my wife, ultimately, sitting me down and stating that she wanted a divorce. In that season, I had been working pretty diligently at growing as a man and a husband, and I had people in my corner who cared and who were cheering for me. Some of those who were made known my wife's statement suggested I pull back so that she could potentially miss what she had.

Respectfully, I declined their suggestions. This wasn't a time to withhold. This was a time to be unconditional, to love her because that is what I desired to do, regardless of her concerns. This was an opportunity to be true to my intentions. If I had pulled back, she could have left believing she was leaving behind the man that I was before and lack the awareness of the man I was truly becoming. Kindness was the answer, to understand her and meet her needs in a season where there was no trust and very little desire to input into our relationship. I believe my allowing her to be honest about how she felt yet remaining true in my kindness and compassion for her allowed some healing into our relationship. Kindness began chipping away at her walls of protection she created due to all that was experienced in the beginning. Trying to protect my feelings would have definitely continued to drive her away. Kindness was a doorway for repentance, a change of mind.

What happens when your love and kindness shows up in your relationships? Does it ever show up? Is this a place where you are lacking in demonstrating love? Are you using worldly methods to combat offenses in your relationship or are you using God's methods? Yes, to operate in loving kindness requires spiritual maturity - the spiritual fruit. Indeed, it is just that, fruit. Like any other fruit, the seed must be planted, it must be nourished, it must endure the seasons, and, once it is produced, it must be given and not wasted. This may not sound easy. There are real challenges. I'm not here to make love seem easy; I'm here to empower you. Without the Spirit, we will continually miss the mark in our relationships. Be wise, not stubborn. Do it God's way. Do you really think your way is better, more promising or safer than God's way? The reality is, again, we have overlooked the purpose and power of kindness.

So when you, a mere human being, pass judgment on them and yet do the same things, do you think you will escape God's judgment? Or do you show contempt for the riches of his kindness, forbearance and patience, not realizing that God's kindness is intended to lead you to repentance? ~ Romans 2:3-4

Kindness is an invitation and a path for your mate's changing mindsets. God could demand and enforce change but He does it through love and kindness. Why? I believe it is because He prefers we function as his children and not as his slaves.

You do not want a relationship full of demands and power struggles. You may get what you want in the moment and lose what you had before that, which was a loving relationship. Kindness leads to opening your mate's heart in hardened areas so that they will be more willing and desiring to make considerable changes all from recognizing the value of the relationship, thus the relationship not only stays intact, but it is strengthened.

As I stated before, this is not easy but it is promising. If it was easy, the divorce rate would not be as high as it is. People, like myself, probably would not be putting out so much effort to assist others with the struggles of maintaining a healthy, flourishing relationship. Marriage counselors wouldn't exist, and the Bible wouldn't include so much information to help and guide us along the way.

Again, for the sake of successful relationships and a healthy love life, we have to learn to follow God's way. Are you operating in loving kindness in your relationships? Are you considering and valuing everything that makes them who they are in this season? Are you kindly meeting the needs of their current circumstances? Are you using kindness to fight off the offenses and hurt, trusting that as God said he'd reward you for feeding the hungry enemy, surely He'll reward you in your relationship, too?

Be more aware of God's kindness in your life, and I believe it will allow you to operate more in kindness. This is a spiritual attribute of someone who is aware and is genuinely appreciative of what God has done for them in his life. This spiritual attribute also requires us to lean on God for help and guidance to rightfully operate in it, but we can do it. As the scriptures said it should, does kindness define you?

It Matters

Whatever your concerns are, whatever you need means so much to me. I desire so much to meet even your smallest request.
Cook your favorite meal after a long day, watch the kids so you'll have a way to relax for a little while. I smile when you're fulfilled. I must confess.
Even when you hurt me, I overcome the pain. Even when you upset me, I find the strength to restrain a reaction, I find greater satisfaction in communicating that I still care.
No matter what we face, it is your face that I still desire to see. There is no place I want to be and not be able to also see you there.
I don't ever want you to ever believe your thoughts and feelings have become irrelevant. God placed a beautiful spirit inside of you; you're heaven sent. You have angels checking in on our conversations.
The power behind your words in my life is evident. The simplest of your statements, to me, is eloquent, so I listen we deep concentration.
Because I want all of your needs fulfilled and at the cost of me I will give all that I can to contribute.
Praying that God will fill in the rest, whatever it takes to remind you that you're blessed. The best thing to ever happen to me, unconditionally, to your everything, I salute.

CHAPTER 3:
Love Does Not Envy

A heart at peace gives life to the body, but envy rots the bones. ~ Proverbs 14:30

Envy - a feeling of discontent or covetousness with regard to another's advantages, success, possessions, etc.

    As much as the Bible tells us what love is, it is also important to know what love isn't. In this scripture, I'd like to think of "the body" expressed here is all of the functions of a person or relationship. Peace allows all components to function in vibrancy and life: the mind, the heart and the soul. The communication, the intimacy and the problem solving are all functioning and are healthy. As the bones serve as the support and protection of all of our body parts, envy rots every function of ourselves and our relationships at its core. The support and protection is rotten. From its definition, it should be very obvious that love does not envy. Lust envies. Basic principle: Love desires to give. Lust desires to receive.

Envy is a feeling of covetousness, to have or receive what others possess. In effect, we say "Give me what you have." Here is the crazy part. As much as many of you would say that this is obvious and definitely not new information, we still allow envy to parade around in our hearts and in our relationships. Here's how we envy or how we allow envy to present itself in our hearts and our relationships.

- We envy when we place more value on the thing or experience we presently covet and overlook the value of the things or experiences we currently possess. We see other couples traveling and overlook the moments we can invest in at home, while at the grocery store and just throughout our day-to-day. We see couples driving nice cars and omit the value of the person in our car seat. These subtle desires and focuses rot the support needed in our relationships.
- We envy when we open the door for resentment towards whatever we perceive is the reason we don't have the things or experiences we wish we had. "I used to be able to go out when I wanted, but I can't because of your expectations in this relationship." "I want to be able to do whatever I want to do with the money I make but marriage says its 'our' money."

We really aren't mad that others have it; we're upset that we don't. That is the difference between envy and jealousy. We envy the "good ole days." We envy the single ladies and gentlemen who parade around in their "freedom found in solitude." Envy makes it seem like you are being denied privilege, but ultimately you're given up the focus on self. Respectfully, get out of your feelings. Get off self.

My friend and I were both performers, poets to be precise. We both had worked hard to establish a name and a following. It seemed like he was excelling faster and more effectively than I. He was getting the big breaks. I was happy for him, but at the same time, it made me look at what I considered to be my lack of success. On top of that, his girlfriend was very supportive and a very visual advocate for him. In churches, wives being helpmates is a message popularly communicated. At the time, I toiled between balancing being there for my wife and child and working hard on my artistic craft.

> Envy is a gateway to more sin.

I begin to resent my wife because I felt that she wasn't as supportive. I felt like she did not want to see me be successful. Ultimately, I stopped viewing us as teammates on the journey. During one argument, envy, which led to resentment, even allowed me to tell her that if I had to choose between her and these dreams of mine, it would be my dreams. In my anger and selfishness, I honestly believed every word of that statement. I was speaking from a selfish place. Of course, I believed those words at the time.

I can tell you, now that I have been focused more on God and the things that my spirit values, that statement is the furthest from the truth. I identified my value in achieving those dreams. However, as I turned to God, he gave me new desires for my heart, and the most valuable of them are far from being focused on self. I can also tell you that removing envy enabled me to see all that my wife was and all that we actually had seven during that season.

Those who belong to Christ Jesus have crucified the flesh with its passions and desires. Since we live by the Spirit, let us keep in step with the Spirit. Let us not become conceited, provoking and envying one another.
~ Galatians 5:24-5

And with this scripture, I'm going to start sounding redundant. Just as upholding love requires the Spirit, refraining from doing what isn't love requires the Spirit as well. The Spirit is the one-stop shop. Continuing to operate in envy is, unfortunate for some, a sign of spiritual immaturity.

And I, brethren, could not speak to you as spiritual people but as to carnal, as to babes in Christ. I fed you with milk and not with solid food; for until now you were not able to receive it, and even now you are still not able; for you are still carnal. For where there are envy, strife, and divisions among you, are you not carnal and behaving like men? ~ I Corinthians 3:1-3

So how can the Word of God show us how to love unconditionally if we are still envious? How can the Spirit direct us in communication if we are still directed by selfish agendas? How can relationships thrive when we are too busy focusing on things outside of our relationships? We have to grow up. We have to spiritually mature. We have to stop envying. It is rotting our bones, the structural support of the way we function in our lives. I really want this to hit home. Don't just skim through the scriptures. Don't minimize the Word. Love does not envy! Don't do it! Envy kills!

Resentment kills a fool, and envy slays the simple.
~ Job 5:2

You can dismiss the dangers of envy if you want to, but you will not have a healthy relationship with it. Even outside of your relationship, you, personally, will never live in peace.

For where envy and self-seeking exist, confusion and every evil thing are there. ~ James 3:16

"Every evil thing are there." I am not the smartest man in the world, but that definitely doesn't sound like a place I want to be. But what does that mean? How is every evil there?

Envy is a gateway to more sin. Envy enough, you'll never believe how much evil you will welcome into your heart: jealousy, hatred, resentment, strife, lust, deceitfulness... And what will you allow yourself to do under such influence of such energy!

My envy was a doorway to entertaining women who offered their support in areas I felt my wife wasn't supporting. I desired so much to fill that desire that I turned to things I never imagined I'd do after I stood at the end of that isle to take her hand in holy matrimony. I gravely wish I could redo that season, but it remains a hard look in the mirror to be exposed to what my flesh is truly capable of doing.

After Adam and Eve took upon the forbidden fruit, do you realize that the first sin was committed from the presence of envy? Cain was upset that God simply looked with favor upon Abel for his offering and did not do so with his. Since he envied Abel and his favor, he killed him. Envy became jealousy which led to murder. Every evil thing is in envy; therefore, love does not and would never envy.

Not Worried About It

I don't have time to focus on what they have. I have much more of a priority to focus on where we are going.
It is not a competition. I'm not keeping up at the Joneses.
I'm just elevating this love for you that is growing.
I don't even look towards the past. I'm past dwelling on the childhood memories. Every day I see you gives me new hope.
Every experience we have adds value to us, even the bad experiences coupled with trust promises riches if through the hard times we learn to cope.
Envying greatness never allows me to rise to the occasion. It's persuasion normally drives the worst out of us.
We must look inside of each other to see the best and put faith in the organs inside of our chests. The joys we will experience will be robust.
I just trust God and believe that in every season he gives us what we need. We never have to live in a spirit of lack.
Even when I dreams are yet realized, we can still experience hope when we look into each other's eyes and appreciate how we have each other's backs.

Because I love you is the only fact that matters. The rest of life that materializes is just chatter. My satisfaction is predicated on your joy.
Not worried about what anybody else in this world gets to do. I'm forever blessed that I get to love you. It is an eternal gratification that I choose to employ.

CHAPTER 4:
It Does Not Boast

Likewise, the tongue is a small part of the body, but it makes great boasts. Consider what a great forest is set on fire by a small spark. The tongue also is a fire, a world of evil among parts of the body. It corrupts the whole body, sets the whole course of one's life on fire, and itself set on fire by hell.
~ James 3:5

The tongue and boasting are an evil threat to oneself and to relationships. We will talk about why love doesn't boast, the dangers of boasting and what boasting looks like.

Boast - to speak with exaggeration and excessive pride, especially about oneself.

Remember, love is purely the substance of desire for the good of someone else. It identifies the value or worth of someone and then proceeds to commit acts to acknowledge and affirm that value. Love in affect says, "I do these things because you are worth it to me." One of the issues with boasting is that you begin to place greater value on you and your acts than on the one that you do them for.

"I work. I buy you nice things. I take you out to eat." "I clean up the house. I iron your clothes. I encourage and support you." "I... I... I..."

When we make statements like these, we communicate to ourselves and our counterparts that they should be grateful for us as opposed to communicating that we do it because we desire to and because we love them and see their worth. Love may know all the things it is doing as an expression of itself, but it will go further and say, "is there more that I can do?" It doesn't spend time glorifying its acts; it presses towards the call.

Jesus performed the greatest act of love. He died for our sins. And though he came back and revealed himself to his disciples, he didn't stop there. He could've spent time boasting about what he had done, but instead he in affect said, "I can do more." He went to the father to intercede on our behalf. He even left the people he loved so that they could be given a Comforter to dwell inside of them. Jesus had every right to stop at, "I died for you." He didn't boast in it, but decided to do more. He said, "You are worth more to me."

I believe we start off in our relationships with similar motivations. We desire the world for them, because "we love them." And while we are exposed to their value, we are also exposed to their faults and shortcomings. Because of the hurt and frustration, we start questioning their value and worth. In this, boasting is afoot. We begin to place greater value on ourselves and our acts than the person who we do them for.

For it is by grace you have been saved, through faith and this is not from yourselves, it is the gift of God - not by works, so that no one can boast. ~ Ephesians 2:8-9

My prayer is that, in our relationships, we operate with a "you can't earn my love because it is a gift" type of attitude. Recognize that, as God freely gave us love, not based on our performance, we don't withhold our love based on performance either. We see in this scripture that boasting has a danger in working in two ways: We may boast in our works or we may boast that we deserve works done for us.

Another danger in boasting in our relationships is that we lose appreciation for what someone is doing for us because we believe we are entitled to those things. I don't want you to walk in low self-esteem, but know that anybody who chooses to genuinely love you has given you a gift that you cannot earn.

For all have sinned and fall short of the glory of God, and all are justified freely by his grace through the redemption that came by Christ Jesus. God presented Christ as a sacrifice of atonement, through the shedding of his blood - to be received by faith. He did this to demonstrate his righteousness, because in his

forbearance he had left the sins committed beforehand unpunished - he did it to demonstrate his righteousness at the present time, so as to be just and the one who justifies those who have faith in Jesus. Where, then, is boasting? It is excluded. Because of what law? The law that requires works? No, because of the law that requires faith.
~ Romans 3:23-27

From this scripture, we see that "all have sinned." You can't boast in your worth. You, too, will cause hurt and frustrations in your relationship. You, too, will fail, even in your best efforts, and disappoint from time to time. By works, you are nowhere in position to demand love, neither can your mate rightfully earn the things you do out of love. Can your relationship survive by the law of works? No! In this boasting is excluded. It has no place.

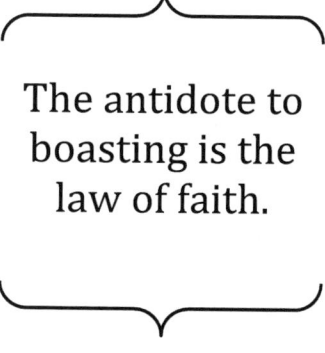

The antidote to boasting is the law of faith.

You may be saying, "I haven't hurt him like he's hurt me" or "I haven't hurt her like she's hurt me." The reality is you could go tit for tat in all of your relationships and they'd all fail, because with this mindset, you're only allowing yourself to play on two roles: the one that's doing more of the hurting or the one that is being hurt more. I, personally, do not want to wear either title. Why are we so focused on the hurting? I get it. Nobody wants to be hurt. As we've talked about before, the hurt is a part of the maturity, the growth, and even the strengthening of the relationship.

WHAT IS LOVE

Jesus didn't want to suffer, either. He wasn't happy about it to say the least. In fact, he wanted out, too, but love and purpose motivated him to endure. He suffered greatly for the things we'd done and even would do afterwards. In effect, he said "This pain is temporary; eternal separation from you is eternal suffering." I don't have time to boast in what I'm doing because I'm on a mission to communicate how much I love you and how much I desire to be with you.

The tongue and boasting are a great evil. Together, they communicate the opposite of what love is trying to communicate. The Bible says, it corrupts the whole body. Your whole identity and your relationship is corrupted. The moment you try to justify yourself in works, you've become the fire that destroys the forest. You begin to tear down the relationship. Why? Because you begin to harden your heart. You begin to strain the ability for love to purely function through you.

The antidote to boasting is the law of faith. Faith requires believing in what isn't seen. Faith requires believing in what will come to pass. Boasting commits acts in self-confidence. Faith commits acts in confidence of someone else.

Those who trust in their wealth and boast in the multitude of their riches, none of them can by any means redeem his brother. ~Psalms 49:6-7

Do not boast about tomorrow, for you do not know what a day may bring. ~ Proverbs 27:1

I planted the seed, Apollos watered it, but God has been making it grow. So neither the one who plants nor the one who waters is anything, but only God, who makes them grow. ~ I Corinthians 3:6-7

Have you given your relationship over to God? Married people, have you given your spouse over to God? Single people, are you giving your dating experiences over to God? Have you placed your faith in Him, truly? The Bible teaches us that faith without works is dead. Are you proceeding in your relationships remembering that you chose to love this person, that God revealed both their worth and your desire to love them? Are your acts a testimony of your faith or simply the conditions of the "contract of works: 'I'll do for you as long as you are doing for me'?" Remember, you cannot earn love. It is a gift. You mate cannot earn your love. It is your gift to them.

This is what the Lord says, "Let not the wise boast of their wisdom or the strong boast of their strength or the rich boast of their riches, but let the one who boasts boast about this: that they have the understanding to know me, that I am the Lord, who exercises kindness, justice and righteousness on earth, for in these I delight."
~Jeremiah 9:23-24

Remember the Bible says that it impossible to know God and not know love, and the only boasting permissible is that of saying you know him. He delights in exercising kindness, justice and righteousness. Do you delight in it?

No Competition

The only thing needed to justify all of my actions is that you're worth it. I work with whatever God has blessed me with to bless you.
With all of your flaws you're still perfect. If love was ever lost on this earth I'd search it to bring it back to you because loving you is something I get to do.

It's never done out of obligation except that I feel obligated to honor my heart and yours.
I must remain true to myself in that loving you is where I accumulate my spiritual wealth, so the things I do for you never feel like chores.
Yet instead the smiles on your face feels like treasures. The joy it places in my heart goes beyond measures. It is my most fulfilling purpose.
I pray God gives me creativity in my future endeavors and that from my heart pride he continues to sever. I believe the things he's allowed me to do for you has only merely scratched the surface.
Yet in still, no matter how many great things I'm gifted to do you will always be held above them. It's no competition.
May they continue to enable you to live, laugh, and love though I feel like I could never do enough, giving you my all will always be my decision.

CHAPTER 5:
It is Not Proud

    I was having a conversation with my wife the other day and something hit me: There is nothing she can do to make me love her more. She could spend her life trying but nothing would directly increase my love for her. The reality is that the only way my love for her could increase is if my spiritual maturity increases. As my spiritual maturity increases, my capacity to love increases and my understanding of how to love becomes clearer.

    As I've mentioned before, the scriptures aren't idle words or suggestions. They describe and provide the commandments of genuine love. It is possible to not recognize genuine love and in return never deliver genuine love because we never learned to stop pursuing love in our flesh. The perversion of love will constantly leave us disappointed and frustrated. We get upset. We grow bitter. Our hearts harden. We blame others. We blame God. In a rage we ask, "Why can't I experience real love?" And God, in all concern and compassion, simply asks, "When will you do it My way?" "I created galaxies. I formed this world and all of the wonders of it. I've created every human being with great intricacy and detail, and you don't trust that I've created and modeled the successful way to love someone and be loved by them?"

To anybody struggling in their marriages, God says it doesn't have to be this way. Surrender your heart and will to Him. Let Him guide and direct you as a husband or a wife. Husbands, there is nothing to be proud of when you have a hurt and lonely wife at home. Wives, your hardened hearts crush the very virtue you were fashioned in. Let it go, and let God do His thing.

My single people, don't let this world define love for you. Let me save you some trouble. They got it wrong. God's way may not seem as exciting, but the "excitement" the world is offering you is full of disappointment, foolish behavior and diminished character.

> **Love has no place for pride.**

I hope you all are truly walking with me. Each day, I get to witness myself love my wife more and more. I can't even accurately describe how fulfilling it has been. As God begins to peel back the veil from your eyes so that you can see your significant other just as He sees them. Beautiful is an understatement. It is enough to make a man cry tears of joy and gratitude. It brings you low in awe and amazement. It establishes genuine intimacy, and the crazy thing about it is that we haven't even arrived yet.

In my studies on the proud and pride, let me tell you, God does not take lightly to proud people. There are extensive examples in the Bible, in fact, too many to reference here. I'll leave this scripture right here, though:

Everyone proud in heart is an abomination to the Lord; though they join forces, none will go unpunished.
~ Proverbs 16:5

"None will go unpunished..." I definitely do not want to be on Team Proud - an abomination to the Lord meaning greatly disliked. God loves us all, but the proud he strongly disliked. I don't know of anybody who desires to be strongly disliked by God. The truth is, however, that pride has driven many of us, if not all of us at some point in time, to be "an abomination to the Lord." Let's dive into this chapter and reveal what pride is, how it affects relationships, and why love will have no part in it.

Proud - having, proceeding from or showing a high opinion of one's own dignity, importance or superiority.

Some of us are pretty familiar with this definition. Where this accurately defines pride, I want us to also look at this scripture:

For behold, the day is coming, burning like an oven, and all proud, yes, all who do wickedly will be stubble.
~Malachi 4:1

So let me help some of us out, here. In this text a word has been defined: "all proud, yes, all who do

WHAT IS LOVE

wickedly..." So when I look at both definitions, I get that proud people are led to do evil things. Does that sound like an extreme conclusion to you? Well, let me ask you this question: What good thing have you even done in your pride?

I looked through the scriptures and found a number of things the proud did or attempted to do. Guess what? It was all evil. David said the proud "have me in great derision," which is to say they have me as the object of mockery. Have you ever, in your pride or sense of being better than your mate, talked about them as if they were foolish in their thinking or actions? Did you publically or in conversation with another scorn them or put them down over a situation? Have you ever had them in great derision? And I get it. Maybe they did in fact do something foolish, but who hasn't? Did you forget your own foolishness at some point in time. See, pride says or makes you believe you are, for the moment at least, superior.

In another scripture, David says the proud has "forged a lie against me." Have you ever been in an argument with a significant other or perhaps a dispute and you withheld information from a confidant or mediator to press your side of the argument? Some of us have just blatantly lied about the scenario because our pride says, "I can't be wrong." "That makes them better than me." "I'll lie on them before I appear to be at fault in this situation." Oh, pride. It sounds a little wicked to me.

The scriptures go on and on. "The proud has risen against me." "The proud digs pits for me." "The proud oppresses me and despises me." In our relationships, in our pride, in taken offense, we set out to get even. For a season or two, we make the one we say we love our enemy, our target to attack to reaffirm our sense of being. "You can't do that to me and think you're going to get away with it." "You can't talk to me any kind of way and think I'm going to care about your feelings." "Do you not know who you are talking to?" "I am me!" Pride.

The person we're supposed to love, we walk around despising. It is no longer about the offense either. It is about how the offense made us feel - less than, the opposite of superior. And you may be trying to justify it by saying I don't desire to be superior, just equal, but did you just assume that you always treat them as equal? I mean equal in every area of your relationship? In your finances? In your intelligence? In your display of love? In your spirituality? You are telling me you've never looked at them as inferior and talked about them or treated them as less than? It is likely that you have, but you are not concerned about it when your pride is on the line.

Pride is wicked. Again, the proud digs pits for me. We can despise our mates so much in pride that we will set them up to fall. "We'll see how productive he is today when I let him oversleep." "We'll see how much she gets done when I cut her off from the money." "Let me withhold love so that you can see just how sorry you are without me." All the proud, yes, all who do wicked... We have to get ourselves together. Pride is nothing to have pride in. Unfortunately, it comes so naturally. No good thing comes out of pride. We have to be wise enough to call on God to help us humble ourselves. Though most humbling moments do not feel good, the results of pride are far more detrimental to our hearts, our lives and our relationships. Here are some things that come out of pride.

Conflict: *He who is of a proud heart stirs up strife...*
~Proverbs 28:25
You'll quarrel with your significant other. Your flesh struggles with your spirit. Your spirit says, "Aren't we supposed to be loving them?" Your flesh responds, "Aren't they supposed to be respecting us?" If pride rules enough, we can't even love when we want to love.

Shame: *When pride comes, then comes shame...*
~Proverbs 11:2
Remember, pride is merely an opinion of self (key emphasis on opinion). Time and circumstance have a way of making the proud feel foolish. You thought you'd feel good if they hurt, too, but now you don't know how to repair the damage. The fact that they cry at the thought of you, at the thought of "us," makes you feel less than a man, less than a woman. How could you let your sense of self take things this far? Was it worth it? Shame - that moment the spirit speaks and reveals the filth you've laid in for some time, the mud on your face, the dirt on your hands, when light exposes your imperfections to the people who bought into your superiority, your self-righteousness.

Destruction: *Pride goes before destruction...*
~Proverbs 16:18
What have we let pride destroy in our lives? How many of us have felt destroyed from our pride? The marriage divorced, the child who now says you were never there, the God that asks, "What have you done?" The people who trusted you to reflect the image of God now hate Him because He made you. What business has failed because of your pride? What dream died in your pride? I could go on and on.

If it is not obvious yet, there is a reason love is not proud. Remember, God is love. Pride dismisses God's presence and influence in a situation.

The wicked in his proud countenance does not seek God; God is in none of his thoughts. ~ Psalms 10:4.

For all that is in the world - the lust of the flesh, the lust of the eyes, and the pride of life - is not of the Father but of the world. ~I John 2:16

See, love, genuine love, is not proud. It won't stand alone from God - superior in its own state. At the beginning of this chapter, I told you love is possible, but we have to do it God's way. In our pride, however, we think we can do it our way and achieve the same results. Real love says, "God, I need you to help me love her the way you have called me to love her." Real love says, "God, I need your help to love him the way you have instructed me to love him." "There is no better way than yours. Fill me with your Spirit, now."

Remember, love desires to give - to benefit the one you love at the expense of self. Love isn't feeding the homeless because they are less fortunate. Love is feeding the homeless because, despite their circumstances, they are worth a well-prepared meal, and love treats it as an honor to serve them. They are still children of God. Why do you think God says, "As you have done to the least of these, you have done also to me? (Matthew 25:40)"

Your spouse isn't lucky to have you; you are blessed to be privileged to serve God by serving the heart and needs of His child. You have no superiority. As you do to your spouse, you have done unto God. Is there one who can say, "Look God at what I've done for You. You owe me?" No, not one can.

God, thank you for putting my place in the right perspective. Humble me. Help me to love as you have commissioned. Thank you for the opportunity. I don't have to do this; I get to do this.

Humble Me

Humble me. We have no reason to think so highly of ourselves. God it is you who keeps us together.
How could we master love within ourselves? Daily our spirits needs your help to witness our expressions of love get better.
It's difficult to not desire to be celebrated. I've waited my entire life to feel like somebody.
Considering all of the times I stumble and fall, it remains evident that you deserve all of the credit. I'm indebted. I saw the bill still you said you got me.
Yet pride seems to always wreak its ugly agenda. To lift myself high, I offend her. Why do I give in to this foolery? I regret it every time I do it. This false sense of worth I seem to pursue it. I'm supposed to overcome it but its ruling me.
So humble me. Help me be a better version of myself. I no longer want to continue in sin.
Help me to heal all of the wounds. The day to be released from pride can't come too soon. Then, I believe our hearts can mend.

CHAPTER 6:
It is not Rude

It is amazing to think of all the things we know not to do in our relationships, yet we still do them. We know we shouldn't have talked that way, replied in that manner, disrespected them, demeaned them, lied to them, and the list goes on and on. These things seem to be so common in our relationships. But why? How are we okay with doing wrong in our relationships? Are we justified by the actions of our mates? Is it because society doesn't say it is that bad? Are we so selfish that we place pride, ego and control over the value of our relationships and the people in our relationships? Is it a lack of self-control? Is it a weakness? A lack of maturity? Again, how do we continually contribute so much wrong into the things we claim we value? How foolish can we continue to be? When will we say it is enough? When will we desire to change? When will we fight to change?

Have we mistakenly considered our actions as minor offenses? Have we validated ourselves with the claim that our good outweighs our bad to the point we feel no guilt for our wrongs - no conviction? Are we so hurt and broken that it fuels our rage, our deadly weapons we use to destroy the things and the ones we say we love? Are we taking our relationships for granted? Has time dulled our view of the beautiful people we're blessed to be with?

When are we going to change? When are we going to do better? Lord, I want to do better. I want to be better. The wrong way is never a good thing. I never want to settle for less than the best - to give my all. I don't want to continue doing things I know I shouldn't do. How could I ever discover other things that I should do better if I don't work to change the things I know not to do? I realize that people in healthy relationships didn't get lucky and find the right one; they were convinced to do it the right way with the one they are with. Show me the way. Show us the way and give us the strength and conviction to follow. I will no longer settle for any wrong I'm doing - no room for excuses! I got to get this right!

In I Corinthians 13, it talks about so many things love is not, so many things that love wouldn't do. As in the previous chapters, we've discussed that love does not boast, envy or be proud, yet we discovered just how common boasting, envying and being proud live within our relationships, and we still question why our relationships aren't thriving. We wonder why or how we managed to fall out of love. I'm convinced that these ill-behaviors and attitudes, that are contrary to love, takes us out of the spirit of love.

I Corinthians 13:5 states that "love is not rude (AMP)," "does not behave rudely (NKJV)," and that "it does not dishonor others (NIV)." Now, before diving into this material, I imagine that, if I polled people in relationships and marriages and asked if they believed they were rude to their significant others, I would receive an overwhelming response of "no" from some. It makes sense to get that response, too. Who views themselves as being rude to their mates? I, also, imagine that I'd get some that would say or admit to being rude at times, perhaps when "provoked." These people aren't proud of it yet aren't shameful enough to be convicted in their hearts to focus on changing. It is like the person sitting on the couch, eating fast food and ice cream, in between bites, saying, "I'll like to get healthy one day." It is not that I don't believe they desire to, but the convicted in heart would get up, throw the junk food away and go for a quick run outside to burn off what they'd already consumed. Desire alone doesn't bring change or results. Conviction does.

    For those who readily state that you are in fact rude to your mate, I see that grim smirk on your faces, entertained by the memories and feelings you get in those moments masked by a false sense of shame. You've placed the majority of the blame on your mate, due to personality differences, past conflicts, or their own attitudes, but how does their identity control you? If you treat them rudely, know that it comes from no other place than that of you being rude in your own heart. No one can draw anything out of you that doesn't dwell within. So, have you been rude to your significant other? Are you rude-natured? Let's take a look and let you make up your own mind.

WHAT IS LOVE

Now, when I looked up the definition of rude, there were some variant definitions of rude, and the artistic side of my brain thought, "Cool, I'll draw out some metaphors and connect them to relationships." However, I later decided it was more important to focus on the one that the author of the scripture was more than likely focused on: being discourteous or impolite, especially in a deliberate way: a rude reply.

I read somewhere recently, and to be specific, it was a book by Ed Cole called *Communication, Sex and Money*. He said that the spirit in which words are given is released as they are spoken. What kind of spirits have been released in your relationship's atmosphere? Sarcastic, belittling, taunting, harsh, bitter, demeaning and/or blunt words have no place in a healthy relationship. And let me say, quickly, that there is a difference between blunt and direct words. You can be direct and still have a tone that considers the welfare of the one being addressed but not when being blunt. The truth without love is mean; love without the truth is meaningless.

We must understand that what we say always indirectly communicates something else as we say it, whether good or bad!

> **The truth without love is mean; love without the truth is meaningless.**

Sarcasm: a sharply ironical taunt; sneering or cutting remark...

...sounds pretty unloving to me. And, yet, the further irony is that I responded to the definition of sarcasm in a sarcastic way. Now, did anybody who fluently speaks sarcastically feel good about being sarcastic when I spoke sarcastically about you being loving in your relationship? I'm pretty sure none of you will. And of course, I don't want to support you being sarcastic so I do not want to encourage you to do it, and I don't want to overlook you doing it, but I can and should communicate my stance on sarcasm without dishonoring or shaming you - the thing that love says it doesn't do. I should've simply said that sarcasm doesn't speak in love at all. I should have said that I trust that I believe you want to communicate in a more loving way and that I believe eliminating sarcasm is a great step forward, and that I believe you can take it. With all of that being said, I just hope you guard yourself from damaging your relationships, especially those relationships you care about the most.

I'm sure you meant no harm in it, most of you, anyway. You might even say that you are just joking when you speak in that way. You believe it is just a little humor. Here's the thing, however; you have placed your significant other at the butt end of that humor - that's never a pleasant place. Another thing is that it may not seem like much when you are just joking around but that same sarcasm also comes out during disputes, which normally erupts those disputes into arguments. When all of that happens, it damages the chances of finding resolutions.

As I mentioned before, being direct with a tone and choice of words considerate of the one you're talking to will go much further than using sarcasm in communication. Sarcasm is just rude.

Belittle: to regard or portray as less impressive or important than appearances indicate; depreciate; disparage.

Why do we keep up this "You ain't all that" attitude with the one we are with? What kind of false sense of protection is that offering us? And what does that say about dating someone we don't consider to be all of that? What does that say about us marrying them. My wife is all of that! Her being all of that in my eyes is motivation for me to honor my role in the relationship. The moment I stop considering her as being all of that is the moment I begin to withdraw my best from her. Who says, "My spouse isn't all of that, but I want to give her [him] my best."

We act as if it is not safe to fully celebrate their worth. "Your speech was okay." "You look okay in that outfit." Where's the "Your speech was powerful!" Where's the "You look amazing!" See, we think because we didn't criticize we didn't belittle, but convincing your mate that they are just okay, just mediocre, is belittling to me.

We convince them that they are less impressive or important to us, especially if they have ever heard you sing praises to someone else. And men (women too), if your eyes aren't wide with wonder when you look at your woman, don't you glance at and/or compliment another woman. That's rude. That's belittling. And I'm not condemning any of you for it; this was a lesson I had to learn for myself. I believe a man who effectively communicates how enamored he is by his woman's beauty can openly communicate that another woman is beautiful, respectfully. If his words and actions constantly demonstrate how impressive and important his woman is, she will not be put off by the simple acknowledgment of someone else, again, if done respectfully. It is still rude to sit, stare and lust after another no matter how much you compliment your mate. That's impolite.

Some of us actually belittle in more intense ways. Again, I strongly question what our motives are when we allow any of these things to happen without sincerely apologizing and turning from the mindset that allowed us to do it in the first place. Pride, ego and power-lust play crucial roles in making severely belittling statements. If you ever find yourself making statements that cut deep, you should search your heart to reveal what is drawing that out of you. Remember, it is coming from somewhere within, not without. Jesus taught that it is not what goes into a man's mouth that defiles him, but what comes out of it, for what comes out comes from his heart (Matthew 15:11).

Love values its recipient. It would never desire to portray him/her as anything less than significant. And as I was writing this, a light bulb hit me, a lot of the time we take their disappointing actions and we degrade the value of a person. Our image of that person begins to reshape. We find less reasons to invest in them. However, here is something to keep in mind. When Jesus was moving forward with his ultimate act of love, he considered not our sins but God's glory and desire for us. He remembered that God breathed on us and placed something of value on the inside. He was not going to allow sin nor death to separate God from that glorious treasure! And so it is, when we are faced with disappointment, we are to remind the people we love of who they are, especially in Christ. Don't reduce them to the act committed.

Here's a good example. Ladies, your man hasn't quite found a job. He's beginning to lose stride in his searching, and he's not doing anything around the house. I get it. That can be extremely frustrating. That has to be an attack on your sense of security. But guess what, he is already beat down and discouraged. He's

WHAT IS LOVE

close to if not already feeling defeated. In frustration, you know what your words and actions call him? Sorry. So now, he further walks into it. Now, he's even mad at you. You were his last chance of finding hope outwardly for what he couldn't currently find inwardly. Had your words and actions referred to him as your man, the one you believe in, the one you sacrifice for because you've seen greatness when you looked at him - I mean, that's why you got with him, right? Remind him; don't belittle him.

And men, you are out there facing the world, taking the blows of the day, the stress of the night, the anxiety of the morning. You're fighting your self-doubt, the natural odds that may be, and your woman seems checked out and oblivious to the whole war that's taking place. She's not cheering for you. She's not fighting for you. I get it. You're disappointed. She's not supplying you with what you need. You feel like you might as well be taking on the world alone, but this is not the time to belittle her. She's already detached and feeling insignificant; don't treat her as such. That's rude. Remind her of the power she possesses. Tell her, "Baby, when you encourage me, look at me like you believe in me, I'm ready to take on the world. Please don't deny me the treasure that is found in your touch, in your soft words, in your motivating energy. I want to bring the world to you because, in my heart, you deserve it. When you actively show me that you believe I can do it gives me the strength to keep fighting for it." Don't be rude. Don't belittle her. Love her. Honor her. Remind her of the value and influence she has in your life.

Harsh: ungentle and unpleasant in action or effect.

Another relationship slayer. When your relationship becomes as hard and brittle as the external elements of life, it is difficult to maintain your buy-in. Harsh words eat away at the gentle comfort that should be found in relationships. Yet, as I mentioned before, we allow these rude acts and words to flow without any self-control and without any regard to the value of our relationships and the one we commissioned to love.

"Move out of the way!" "Shut up!" "You are so stupid!" "Get out of my face!" "I don't want to be bothered with you!" "You make me sick." "I hope you die and go to hell." "I can care less about what you have to say." "I can care less about how you feel." "So what!" We've either been guilty of saying these things or the victim of hearing these things. And in the heat and frustration in which these words are usually given, they drive love and intimacy further from our relationships. The Bible teachers that the power of life and death are in the tongue (Proverbs 18:21). Why do we allow ourselves to choose death? We are literally killing our relationships and the heart of the one we claim to love!

What's even further disheartening is that the same spirit within us allows us to even talk to our children that way. How can we be content with stripping the gentleness of our relationships with harsh, rude words, bringing shame to our mates for believing that we ever thought highly of them and that we cared? Remember, we indirectly say other things while we talk. Ninety-three percent of communication is non-verbal, yet when harsh words or spoken, however, a hundred percent of the communication is negative! And some of us will say that we get mad because we care so much. Well, if you really care, learn to address them in the right, loving way and stop responding in a way that destroys what you all have!

WHAT IS LOVE

I remember when I realized how rude I had been to my wife. We had returned home following church service and the marriage class we attended after each service. We were dialoguing about the topic for the day in class and she explained to me how harsh my words had been in the past. I'm sure she must have brought it up before, but I hadn't been in a mindset to truly become better for myself and for the marriage. I, honestly, had no idea or genuine insight until then, but I heard her and I believed her in my heart. I acknowledged the truth. I felt immediate sorrow to the point of tears. I responded to the pain and hurt in her eyes. Not only did I apologize, but I made a personal commitment to God, to her and to myself that I would not continue to talk harshly towards her, under any circumstance.

If you, too, have realized that you've been rude to your significant other, I want to give you some spiritual and practical tools I used to repent and change my ways. One of the things I did, and it has become my constant thing to do, is that I asked God to help me see my wife just as He sees her. I believe that when you spiritually view them, you focus on the value they possess, even in the challenging moments.

A practical thing I did was slow down my speech. I made extra effort to think and meditate on the words I was about to speak, considering ultimately what they truly communicate. I even did this for comments I would make jokingly. I simply asked myself if the words were loving. If they weren't, I either found a better way to say it, or I would choose not to say anything. Keep in mind, this practice must be practiced with the right intentions and goals. I'm not doing these things to simply prevent an argument, though it is hopefully a viable byproduct. I am doing these things to consider her heart, because I care about her and I love her. Trying to avoid an argument will not go the distance, and it will not draw you closer to each other.

Another thing I did was I asked her to help me in the future by letting me know if and when I was being rude. I insisted that I want to know because I want to change.

Love is not rude; it does not behave rudely; it does not dishonor others. Are you polite in your relationship, treating your mate with high regard? Do your words and energy toward them honor them? If not, it will continually leave both a void and a bacteria in your relationship, slowly and painfully infecting and eating away at it. In all your words and responses, consider who your mate is to God and who he/she is to you. How I treat you will speak specifically to who you are to me. If I love you, respect you and honor you, through any season, my words and actions can and will affirm the beauty you carry and the blessing you are.

My Words

When I speak and you hear it, I pray you always receive a loving spirit and nothing less.
I hope my choice words are considerate and a compassionate tone is deliberate. May my words never lead you to stress.
May they be used to bless you and never curse. Before I speak I'll consider your feelings first. May the pillars forever be love and respect.
May I never speak with haste. May the expressions on your face be a guide for my tone to be correct.
May my words never be used to tear you down but build you up. Please speak up if they ever do differently.

WHAT IS LOVE

May my words never cause you sorrow or pain. If they ever trouble you, please give me room to explain my true intentions so that I never become your enemy.
May my words always honor your worth. May each conversation continue to birth new intimacy for all the days that come.
May my words always be honest and true built on the foundation of my love for you. Whenever you are in need of words of affirmation, may always have some.

CHAPTER 7:
It is not Self-Seeking

  What do you look for to determine that you are ready to get married or if you have found the right person to marry? Most people will say that they look for compatibility. It sounds like a smart answer, but what does compatibility really mean? Having a lot in common? Liking each other, equally? Loving each other, equally? Having similar goals? Compatibility may not be what you think it is.

  How do you know that you've found the right one? Because they have love for you? I like hearing "because we are equally yoked." That term has been so popularly misconstrued that it isn't even funny. Maybe you say that he/she has good character and morals or that he/she is spiritually sound and driven. Perhaps, it is because you are exceptionally attracted to them, and you have never in your entire history been this attracted to anybody. They must be the one, right? I remember my response when I was asked after the engagement was announced. I simply stated, "I just know. The fact that I am not asking myself that same question, I just know."

I don't believe I was wrong in my response no more than I believe that the aforementioned things aren't important. However, I believe there is an important revelation missing that we fail to acknowledge before making the decision of getting married or in choosing the right mate. I believe this revelation could proactively omit a lot of the initial heartaches experienced during the initial seasons of marriage and even with the ongoing adventures. This revelation has everything to do with what the true condition of our hearts are and our true intentions. This revelation is an indicator of how much love is genuinely in the air.

So moving forward with I Corinthians 13, it says that love is not self-seeking or simply put that love is not selfish. I believe the selfish trait is the most present and the most difficult to eliminate within relationships. I'm not even sure we can ever actually completely eliminate it. I know I haven't; but I'm working on it. And, shame on you, if, right now, you're thinking that you're not selfish in your relationships. But if you are thinking that, it is all good. We're getting ready to talk about it, right now.

Like many of the other elements that we have discussed, selfishness tends to blend with the expected nature of relationships, but the reality is still that selfishness does not belong and never will foster a healthy relationship. So, my focus and concern is that, as you read this chapter, we expose our on selfishness in effort to begin eliminating it. So as we discuss these things, don't be thinking of your mate. Focus on self.

That sounds selfish, but it isn't. We are focusing on self to be a better lover for them.

Now, self and what self focuses on is the fine line between love and lust. And we definitely do not want to view ourselves as lustful. Such blasphemy. This is mainly because we popularly if not solely associate lust with desiring sex, but even outside of sex, we are some lustful creatures, shamefully admitted.

The sad part about it is that lust will at times disguise itself as love. Guys, don't be fooled, you don't have sex with a woman before marriage because you love her so much. That, in any shape or form, is a lie. Sorry, but it is true. Ladies, of course, the same goes for you. I'm not judging those that have because I would also have to judge myself for having pre-marital sex. I only mention it here because I do not want you to be foolishly mislead by a lie. The reality is that love does not desire to do anything bad towards another person and causing someone to dishonor God is definitely in the "doing something bad" category. Of course, God has reasons why he is against it (not just to deny you pleasure), but that is a different topic for a different day.

Anyway, so let us get back to this line: What is love? What is lust? There are two definitions that we are going to use to filter all of our actions and thoughts through to determine whether they stem from love or lust. Is it love or is it lust? Love is the act of benefitting others at the expense of self. Lust is benefitting self at the expense of others. Let the mental gears turn on these for a minute. That's right. Anything that entices you based on what you'll receive is under the motivation of lust. Anything that entices you based on what you will give is under the motivation of love. It may sound extreme but we need to be extreme to genuinely assess our motives. Your relationship will not prosper with you lying to yourself.

"Dang, BJ, so am I wrong to desire to be loved, to be treated right or to have nice things?" The answer is truthfully no, but we're not talking solely about desires, we're talking about motives and the actions and thought life that are birthed from them.

Right now, I want to focus on the word "expense" being used in these definitions. Expense is equivalent to the term "paying a price or cost." With that in mind, lust and love can be differentiated by who bears the cost in your motives and who is getting paid or benefiting. Love requires a fee from you - a cost. The problem is that we are so lust-focused that we get upset with paying fees or we begin to think something is wrong as we pay fees throughout our relationships. In reference to this idea, we become eager to get married when we are persuaded that their love banks are large enough to be spent on us, and we look forward to spending it. However, we rarely assess our own love bank balance because we are not focused on spending it. We become frustrated in our relationships because we believe they aren't spending enough or that we are spending too much. I understand wanting love to be reciprocated, but I want to mathematically point out why these thoughts are lustfully driven.

To make the argument, let's use dollar amounts instead of the traditional percents we usually reference in our input in the relationship. For example, we may say we are putting in seventy percent and they are only putting in thirty percent. Instead, let's say we are putting in seventy dollars and they only put in thirty dollars. Well, that means you've paid forty dollars. The expense falls on you. Congratulations, that is love.

Some of us desire this fifty-fifty relationship. Let's look at that. If I put in fifty dollars and she puts in fifty dollars, I'm not losing or paying anything. We are trading at an even value, which is not a bad thing. However, if I am demanding this even exchange to continue in the relationship, I am not focused on loving her. The last scenario is quite obvious. If we desire to put in less, we are definitely lusting.

For those that are getting discouraged or frustrated, before I lose you, let me make this statement. It is not wrong to communicate needs or desires from your mate. In fact, it is unwise not to communicate these things. In an ideal relationship or in a healthy one, both people are in fact loving each other. Don't be mistaken, though; the unbalanced seasons are natural. You may be giving more right now, but keep on living. You may not even recognize it, but they will be the ones putting in more of the love as you endure trying seasons together. Of course, we want to eliminate as much of the "uneven" seasons as possible, but, again, they are very natural. The issue is not in the communicating your needs and desires. The issue is focusing on them so much that you begin to refrain from loving them or paying your expense for the benefit of them.

> **Lust will disguise itself as love.**

Okay, I still want to point out some ways we are self-seeking, selfish and lustful in our relationships. To do so, I want to reference a few scriptures from the Bible.

WHAT IS LOVE

Sheol (the place of the dead) and Abaddon (the underworld) are never satisfied; nor are the eyes of man ever satisfied. ~ Proverbs 27:20 AMP

If we have a lustful focus in our relationships, the reality is that our mates will never satisfy us. We will always want more. Our relationships will never flourish because, to us, it will always appear to be insufficient. We will continually focus on what we don't have verses what we do have. Use wisdom, today, and acknowledge that our selfishness somehow takes us down and endless road that still mystically leads us to a dead end.

Remember, I said that lust will disguise itself as love in some instances. Oftentimes, we do good things for our mates because we want something in return. We have these intentional barter systems in place. The most common is when men romance their women in efforts to have sex. Sure, we want to keep with the romance theme and use the term "make love." Again, love and lust is determined by the motivation the act is birthed from, not the act itself. We can do "good" things or make "good" requests but they produce no good outcomes. To practically check your motives behind your actions, ask yourself if you will be satisfied if you do not directly benefit from your own actions. If romance only leads to her sleeping well tonight knowing her man loves her, are you okay with that?

The truth is that it isn't only about sex. Sometimes, we do good things because we want the anticipated praise, validation and "pats on the back." We do good things and ultimately the motive is more about feeling good about ourselves than it is about genuinely benefiting the recipients of our deeds. That's still selfish. We do good to build the case and evidence of our self-righteousness and for our own pride. We thrive on being able to say, "Look how good I am." "You should feel good about having me." We may not actually say it out loud, but our attitudes towards the situation and relationship reflect these thoughts. This might be a tough pill to swallow, but we might as well be honest with ourselves and our motives because the outcome will still be a product of whatever is the truth.

Do not be deceived, God is not mocked [He will not allow himself to be ridiculed, nor treated with contempt nor allow his precepts to be scornfully set aside]; for whatever a man sows, this and only this will he reap. For the one who sows to his flesh [his sinful capacity, his worldliness, his disgraceful impulses] will reap from the flesh ruin and destruction, but the one who sows to the Spirit will from the Spirit reap eternal life. Let us not grow weary or become discouraged in doing good, for at the proper time we will reap, if we do not give in. ~ Galatians 6:7-9

You ask [God for something] and do not receive it, because you ask with wrong motives [out of selfishness or with an unrighteous agenda], so that [when you get what you want] you may spend it on your [hedonistic] desires. ~James 4:3

Notice, in these scriptures, God is against granting us anything good when we seek it with selfish ambitions. Men, we cannot establish intimacy in our marriages with sex as our goal. We may luck up some of the time with sex, but we will never reach the potential of true intimacy. Our wives will ultimately resentfully give in or simply check out once they begin to feel pursued as an object. Women, you can't expect your words of encouragement to continue to fulfill him and motivate when accomplishing chores and "honey-do" lists are your true motives. He will actually begin to feel used and unappreciated in the process.

I believe there is a reason the scripture says to not grow weary in well doing. I believe the fruit is delayed to test our motives. If you find yourself getting frustrated in doing good because you are not getting what you want, it may be evidence that your actions aren't coming from the right place. It could also be evidence that you are growing weary and no longer trusting in the good seeds you've planted into your relationship.

I have a friend who came to me at a time he was extremely frustrated concerning his marriage. I've known him for some time, so I can attest that his marriage has been on the forefront of his mind for some years up until this moment. He felt like he had been doing all that he could possibly do to make his marriage work, but he just wasn't getting anything out of his wife. He'd been praying, going to church more often, reading devotionals on his own, trying to do more things around the house and just about anything that he could think to do. He felt like his wife was just not fighting for the marriage or trying to do anything for him. They hadn't had sex in a year. I genuinely believe he had every right to be concerned. Though this chapter is about selfishness, I find it befitting and appropriate to insert this scenario here so that we may all examine ourselves. Had he become selfish or weary? The actual question to be asking is if either of those options are acceptable?

I had sympathy for my friend, however; as a friend, I am compelled to make sure that myself and my friends are always examining ourselves, regardless of our situations. We have authority over our own hearts. What he decided to do in this situation would be by choice and not obligation, regardless of the external "forces" that may be. In my own devotion, I came across this scripture:

I know your deeds and your toil, and your patient endurance, and that you cannot tolerate those who are evil, and have tested and critically appraised those who call themselves apostles (special messengers, personally chosen representatives, of Christ), and [in fact] are not, and have found them to be liars and impostors; and [I know that] you [who believe] are enduring patiently and are bearing up for My name's sake, and that you have not grown weary [of being faithful to the truth]. ~'But I have this [charge] against you, that you have left your first love [you have lost the depth of love that you first had for Me]. ~'So remember the heights from which you have fallen, and repent [change your inner self -- your old way of thinking, your sinful behavior -- seek God's will] and do the works you did at first [when you first knew Me]; otherwise, I will visit you and remove your lamp stand (the church, its impact) from its place -- unless you repent. ~Revelations 2:2-5

My eyes were wide open and my heart was full of energy. Here it is, a church who was doing all of the work yet Jesus had one charge against them: they "left [their] first love" - the depth of love they first had for Him. Now, was I foolish enough to tell my friend, after he had been doing all of those things for his marriage, that he had lost his love for his wife? No. But I did send it to him for him to examine his own heart. He had been fighting for his marriage, which is admirable. Had she became merely a part of the puzzle? A part of an objective - no longer pursued as his "first love" but as a role and duty? Could he pursue her and do for her as he did the moment after they tied the knot? If not, if he didn't return to his love for her, as Jesus promised this church, the impact of his work would be removed. Could his impact have been removed because he began to place too much emphasis on the work and goals and not enough on his love for his wife? Had he subconsciously lost the depth of love that he had for his wife? The answer to that question was not for me to give him. Just like him, we must all pray and ask God to reveal the truth to our spirits in these types of situations.

Now, there are two other ways we are selfish in our relationships that I want to touch on. One of them is that we are selfish in the way we expect things to happen - our way or the highway, my will, not God's will be done. In this way, we are selfishly demanding our mates to function like programmable robots: see things our way and do things the way we believe they should be done. This offers us a certain comfort, control and security we do not want to give up or sacrifice for the sake of the relationship. It is selfish to not consider that there are multiple approaches to things in life and that God has made us differently for a purpose. We lower the value of their views and ultimately our complete buy-in if our mates don't function the way we expect them to because their ways don't seem to benefit us. Preferences become selfishness when we begin to withdraw due to unmet expectations. Since we are not getting our way, we don't want to pay love's fee.

Another way we are selfish is that we want to avoid suffering. Jesus readily knew he'd have to suffer greatly to carry out his act of love. Marriage should reflect Christ's relationship with his church but we never consider suffering greatly for our mates as part of that reflection. Loving unconditionally sounds cute until it is put to the test. Jesus died for our sins, the things we did and would do in the future. In many relationships, trials and tribulations are limited to those we really cannot blame our mates for our suffering: illnesses, accidents, and acts of God. We will have grace for these areas, most of the time. However, let our suffering be directly tied to the actions of our mates, we are ready to leave the relationship, even though, Jesus suffered for our faults. In marriage, we are to die to self. This doesn't sound pleasant and the reality is that it isn't, at least in the season of dying - no more than it was for Jesus. But without death, there can be no resurrection. Jesus' power was greater after death. His example and evidence of who he was came through his resurrection.

I believe, in dying to self, our influences and effectiveness are far greater in our relationships. Single people, this isn't a pass to lower standards, remove boundaries and live haphazardly with someone. This is more of a message to married people, in Holy covenant, to give yourself away to your mates, whole-heartedly, despite the past and despite the current circumstances. Jesus saw our filth and was not afraid or ashamed to love us. In fact, He was honored. Be honored to love your mate, selflessly, as they are. In doing this, you will reap a harvest.

Men, pursue your wives. Affirm their worth through word and deed. Make your hearts sensitive to their cries, concerns, complaints and desires. Serve these areas, righteously. Withhold nothing good from them. Honor their bodies as God's temple. Honor their identities as His daughters. Submit your body to her. There, in due season, you'll find intimacy. There, in due season, we'll discover what it feels like to make love and not just have sex, not just because of their willingness but because our hearts will have finally been corrected in that area - no longer perverted by the lust of our flesh.

Women, honor your husbands. Present yourselves daily, desiring to be the apple of his eyes. Serve him like the king of your home, being sensitive to the weight of responsibility he carries in that role. Offer him comfort because you care, not because you feel obligated to do it. Cover him when he is down. Celebrate him as often and liberally as possible. Then, you'll wake up every day to a knight in shining armor with the strength, courage and passion to sweep you off your feet all of the days of your life.

How do you know you're ready for marriage? How do you know that he/she is the one? Do you desire to be expended at their benefit? Are you convinced that you can die to self to co-communicate the greatest act of love man can communicate? Are your motives driven to give more to them than they are to receive from them? Could you give a hundred percent in seasons where they have nothing to give? And if you're not there yet, do you desire to be there? Being ready for marriage is not about what you have found in them, but what you have discovered about yourself and your own heart, through them. Just remember that love, real love, is never ever self-seeking.

My Reason

I give all I have to you simply because I desire to. You have the same opportunity to return that type of love to me, if you want.
There's something about doing great things for you that pleases me. We can spend an eternity in ecstasy. Failure could never daunt.

The things I give have no strings. You're no puppet. I just love it when love draws us closer.

The time I put in never ends. I replay the memories as records spin. A picture of you satisfied is my favorite poster.

Whatever you need from me I give freely. It would eat me inside to know that I could've helped you in any way yet withheld.

I pray I never let selfishness get in the way. I never want to see the day I see you leave because of, at loving you, I failed.

So whatever I can do I will. Whatever I have is yours. My patience. My support. If you need me to go out on a limb, I bring you back the forest.

In loving you, I'll receive my greatest fulfillment. It's easy to develop this skill when I allow love to lead my spirit. What runs through my veins is not blood but my love for you. My heartbeat plays a special song for you. I hope you hear it every time you come near it.

CHAPTER 8:
It is not Easily Angered

There is a saying: "Play the victim long enough and you'll become the villain." This saying is referring to our mindsets in our relationships. Often times, you can find someone who has been hurt, disappointed, or let down in a relationship, maybe not just once, but perhaps even a few times. Because of this, their hearts and minds begin to focus on the offenses, reliving them in their heads and even anticipating more offenses. Despite whatever other things that are going on in the relationship, the relationship becomes a threat: a threat to happiness, comfort, security, esteem, ... you name it. The other person, currently, is portrayed as the root of the problem - the villain. They are responsible for our sadness and anger. Again, despite their other qualities, despite the fact that these are mere problems, mistakes and disappointments, in our minds, we change their identities and their intentions, and we overall ignore any good in the relationship. If this isn't already over the top and outrageous, it gets worse. Because of our jaded perspective, we begin to resent them, live in the negative and withdraw ourselves.

When things could be pleasant and peaceful, we are harsh, cold and withdrawn. We begin to act out in rage and bitterness. The relationship is now withering, crumbling, perishing and under attack, not because of their actions, but that of our own. We've allowed their few acts to alter our daily character. We have become the villains. It can even be said that our reactions are worse and more detrimental to our relationships than their actions.

And here is why and where we become comfortable with all of this: We feel, in ourselves, justified in our altered stance in the relationship. They offended us. They betrayed us. They wronged us. They disrespected us. We are this way now because of them. In fact, we could be worse; they should feel lucky.

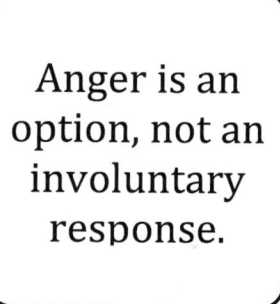

Anger is an option, not an involuntary response.

You know, in America, it is said that we have freedom of speech; however, just because you have a right doesn't make what you say and do right. Just because you have been mistreated, you may have a right to be upset, to get angry, to retaliate, to withdraw, or to withhold, but it doesn't make doing any of this the right thing to do. If you focus on having a right to do it, you'll show no remorse for your actions and perhaps you'll even live comfortably in your "villain" state. If you focus on what's right to do, you may exercise more restraint, and if you perhaps still give in to the desire to react to offenses, you'll acknowledge the wrong, apologize, repent and work to restore the damage.

One of the strongest emotions that contribute to this victim-gone-villain mentality is anger. Anger is defined as a strong feeling of displeasure and belligerence aroused by a wrong, or wrath. To further land it home, belligerent is a warlike or aggressively hostile nature, condition or attitude.

I believe you can be hurt, offended or even upset and not have anger. Anger is an option. You can avoid introducing wrath, war and hostility into your relationship. The moment you welcome it in, you begin to treat a loved one as an opponent, like an enemy. The reality, however, is that though we've offended each other, disagreed, disrespected each other, hurt each other, disappointed each other, or misunderstood each other, we are not enemies; we're friends. We are lovers. We are not opponents; we are on the same team.

In I Corinthians 13, we find that love is not easily angered. And the Bible also has words for those that are easily angered:

Do not be eager in your heart to be angry, for anger dwells in the heart of fools. ~ Ecclesiastes 7:9

Dang, Bible! Anybody feeling like a fool right now? God knows, by my feeling like I had a right to be angry, I've been this foolish on many occasions. It feels so natural to be angry, but we must remember that "natural" state of man, as he is governed by his flesh, is a sinful nature. Spiritual identity and natures are developed. Many things that feel right in our flesh are gravely wrong, and anger, human anger, is one of them.

I mean, let's ask ourselves a question and be honest: Have we ever done something good in anger?

I know some of us actually believe we have actually communicated something good in anger. We believe our showing how angry we really were allowed them to know just how serious we were about the situation. The reality is that our mates may have, in fact, complied or heard us out due to the energy of our anger. I will not disagree with you for the sake of making an argument. I've heard my wife through her anger. Keep in mind, I was praying that I would hear her through her anger as she candidly communicated her concerns. However, I can recall times that we responded negatively to each other's anger as well. So, is anger a good thing? A bad thing? An amoral thing? I've discovered that God has placed conditions on anger - guidelines, what have you.

God is concerned with the ease of being angered, the duration of being angered, the identity of being angered and the acts committed in anger. So, is anger itself sinful? No, but it can be a conduit of sin, so tread very cautiously and controllably in your anger. There's a scripture you may be familiar with:

Be angry [at sin, at immorality, at injustice, at ungodly behavior], yet do not sin; do not let your anger [cause you shame, nor allow it to] last until the sun goes down. ~Ephesians 4:26 AMP

I used the amplified version, intentionally. Some people like to use this scripture to justify any type of anger, but here, you see the author was referencing specific targets of anger. Men, this doesn't justify you being angry that she will not let you watch football all day. Ladies, this doesn't justify you being angry that he won't let you max out the cards on your fashion craves. While I went with stereotypical examples, if you are getting angry over materialistic or selfish ambitions, respectfully, get over that. This selfish anger has no place in a healthy relationship.

Also, in this scripture, you can see that the author separates anger from sin. It instructed us to be angry but do not sin. Essentially, be angry but do not act out in our anger. Again, specifically, it is referring to the anger directed at sin, because you may shame yourself in your own sin. This scripture takes me back to the victim-gone-villain situation. How many times were we unloving because they were unloving to us? They cursed us out so we cursed them. They talked about us to others, so we spoke poorly of them, too. They selfishly withheld something from us, so we withheld something we knew was important to them. Here's the thing: if it was so wrong of them to do it, it is also wrong for us to do it as well. Don't be mistaken. Sin is sin. Immorality is immorality. Ungodly behavior is ungodly behavior. No circumstances can change it. No bad act can justify another bad act.

Lastly, this scripture says to not allow the sun to go down on your anger. We have a deadline to release our anger. Some of us are still angry about things that happened years ago. You have to let go of anger. Remember, anger may not be sin, but it is a conduit of sin. You hold on to anger long enough and it becomes a part of your character and your identity.

Come on. Be honest. You've seen angry people. They walk around like there's nothing to be happy about, people or an annoyance, positivity is a headache. You simply speak to them and they get upset. They are offended about everything. One night, they laid down with anger and when they woke up, they were one with anger.

Some of us have been angry so long, we can't even pinpoint why we became angry in the first place. I used to carry huge chips on my shoulders. All that time I had no peace, no joy, no intimacy. Days, years even, just wasting away, especially in my relationships, and again, I couldn't even tell you how or where it all got started. You know, you look back on all of those moments you acted in anger and thought you made your point. Then, life continues to happen and eventually your eyes open. I know for me, I now see my foolishness in those moments, how I hurt and disrespected people in those moments, how I pushed loved ones away and how I sinned. Acts of anger have no place. Dwelling in anger is a dangerous season.

The Bible gives ample evidence that angry people are no good to dwell with or be around. Proverbs 14:17 says that a quick-tempered man acts foolishly and without self-control. The lacking self-control was one of my main reasons I wanted to get a handle on my anger. A body out of control doesn't desire to do anything good. This is usually the epitome of where one's wrath is demonstrated: yelling, name calling, throwing things, punching walls, or even worse, punching actual people. Some have lost control and have committed murder. Again, the effects of anger is not to be taken lightly. I, from experience, wouldn't recommend lacking self-control or being with someone who lacks self-control. It's hazardous. If you're there, get the help. I know my church and others like it have anger management classes.

WHAT IS LOVE

It is better to live in a corner of the housetop [on the flat roof, exposed to the weather] than in a house shared with a quarrelsome (contentious) woman. ~Proverbs 29:24

Now, perhaps a familiar scripture, but let's analyze that. A man, who is designated the head of the house would rather give up all authority of the home than deal with a woman who wants to fight or war about everything. I've seen it before. She seems to be upset about everything possible - can't get happy. In lieu of trying to resolve the unending list of concerns and problems, she defaults to the "do whatever you want and leave me alone" attitude. He has no control over the weather outdoors he's exposed to but feels he has even less control over the condition of his marriage and home.

Women, there is a better way to communicate your needs and concerns than quarreling and warring with your man. Again, I think one of the easiest things people can do is take a fact, create a false reality and operate in it. He doesn't clean up the kitchen. That is a fact. However, you falsely translate it into "He doesn't care about me." "He hasn't told me he loved in a while." Perhaps a fact, but then you conclude he doesn't love you anymore. That isn't necessarily true. He could believe he is showing it in other ways than words. In his mind, he may not want to overuse it in order to keep it special. Now, I'm not saying that these are healthy things to do, but sticking to the facts without prematurely creating realities allows for discussions of concern verses arguments over whose perceptions or points of views are right. The anger will often be found in the perspective reality and not the simple fact... unless you're already angry. Just remember, arguing angrily excessively is a surefire way to make a man checkout. Men, it goes without saying that you shouldn't be quarrelsome with your wives or girlfriends either.

An angry man stirs up strife, and a hot-tempered and undisciplined man commits many transgressions. ~Proverbs 29:22

In addition to what has already been alarming and concerning, we see many transgressions are the product of someone who is an angry person. How many sins are we going to cause our loved ones to put up with because we choose to be angry about offenses? What type of sins will we commit? Infidelity? Slander? Lying? Acts of pride? Fits of rage? Remember, acting out in anger ultimately leads to shame. Even outside of romantic relationships, parents, you've ever lashed out at your child in frustration and anger because of some annoyance are unmet directive? For those of us who adore their sweet, gentle spirits, to see the joy and innocence leave their faces by the weight of our own words is difficult. It is shameful. We find ourselves returning, in softer tones, apologizing in an attempt to explain the point we were trying to make, now, without the anger.

Likewise, I strongly recommend mastering communicating, without the anger, to our significant others. My wife will not talk to me about things until she's processed her anger. I actually appreciate her for that. What kind of resolution do we really expect to come out of speaking in anger? I'd rather wait until she has settled her anger, and we'll have an easier, more effective time hearing and respecting each other's concerns, thoughts, feelings and overall value.

Now, anger, in itself, is not sin. The Word says love is not easily angered. It did not say that love is

WHAT IS LOVE

never angered. It is impossible to never be angered. The realistic attitude to have is that when we experience anger, quickly remove it.

Let all bitterness and wrath and anger and clamor [perpetual animosity, resentment, strife, fault-finding] and slander be put away from you, along with every kind of malice [all spitefulness, verbal abuse, malevolence]. ~Ephesians 4:31

But now rid yourselves [completely] of all these things: anger, rage, malice, slander, and obscene (abusive, filthy, vulgar) language from your mouth. ~Colossians 3:8

As often as you experience the urge to do any of these things, resist and remove the urge. Proverbs 19:11 states that "good sense and discretion make a man slow to anger, and it is his honor and glory to overlook a transgression or an offense [without seeking revenge and harboring resentment]. (AMP)"

We don't have to say everything that comes to mind to say. We can use good sense. If I want this relationship to work out, should I really be saying this? Even if I currently feel this way? What is my ultimate goal here? I must use good sense before I break down the very thing that I desire to build, all because my emotions got the best of me.

I love the part of the scripture that refers to the honor and glory of overlooking offenses, and I find it to be very true. I made a powerful discovery in my marriage: whatever shortcomings I face due to my wife's transgressions are not as bad as I may naturally view them. God equips my heart to endure them, to cover her and still present her pure, if I allow Him to do so. It is a mighty thing to strive to model the words "nothing can separate me from my love for you." Should she continue in sin, though grace abound? No, but grace is here for her. My grace - as liberally as God has offered me grace. It helps to keep this in my mind, because, though I am not God, I acknowledge that I need His grace and her grace just as much. I have no need or place to harbor resentment or seek revenge. That only comes from a selfish, hateful nature.

    The last thing I want to discuss concerning anger is God's example in his covenant with his people. I want to connect his example to marriage - the representation of his covenant. Now, I'll be honest, there are many scriptures that reference God's anger, so one may view him as a vengeful, wrathful God, especially if you look at the Old Testament. However, you'll discover that only some of those scriptures reference actual statements and acts of anger. Many other scriptures were authored by people who feared experiencing his anger, though they did not actually experience it. However, there are other scriptures, in the Old Testament as well, that provide a more complete picture of God, concerning anger.

But He, the source of compassion and loving kindness, forgave their wickedness and did not destroy them; many times he restrained His anger and did not stir up all His wrath. ~Psalms 78:38

    Likewise, in our marriages, I suggest we exercise compassion and loving kindness despite their wickedness. We may get angry, but restrain it. Restraining our anger keeps our love and care present despite the hurt and offense. In this, we can express disappointment as opposed to expressing wrath.

WHAT IS LOVE

For his anger is but for a moment, but His favor is for a lifetime. ~Psalms 30:5

Let your love for your spouse outweigh the anger of a moment. Let your desire to do well for them outlast the time of anger. Return as quickly as possible to the love you promised to give. Like I have discovered for myself, your love is built to cover their offenses. Yes, all of them.

They refused to listen and obey, and did not remember Your wondrous acts which you had performed among them; so they stiffened their necks and [in their rebellion] appointed a leader in order to return them to slavery in Egypt. But you are a God of forgiveness, gracious and merciful and compassionate, slow to anger and abounding in loving kindness; and you did not abandon them. ~Nehemiah 9:17

Now, let's correlate this to marriage. Your spouse refused to listen to you, hear you out, and obey what you all have agreed to do. They forget about all of the good things you've done for them and the marriage so they choose to leave you. And sure you, like God, were angered but you restrained some of your anger so that they would not be destroyed and so that they would not feel the weight of your wrath. Due to your compassion and lovingkindness, though you were angered, you did not abandon them. You forgave them and kept your covenant. There are so many testimonies of this great example of love living and breathing right now as you read these words. They are powerful examples, through overcoming infidelity, gambling problems, and drug addictions, of love's redemptive spirit. It is definitely not the easiest of things to do, by far, but it is promising!

I know it is a lot to take in, and even far more difficult for some to believe they could overcome all of these things. In your own might, you would be absolutely correct. It is impossible, but if you allow God's love for you to flow through you and into your spouse, it is more than possible.

Love is not easily angered, and when it becomes angered, it restrains the anger and quickly does away with it so that compassion and forgiveness can set in. We're on the same team, let us not war and quarrel with one another like enemies. Fools do that, not lovers. Have self-control in those situations. The Bible says that the person with self-control is mightier than a soldier (Proverbs 16:32). We are truly at war to represent and protect the face of God's holy union. Put on your armor and fight the good fight. God commands it. He honors it, and your spouse is worth it.

Only for a Moment

Only for a moment I could ever take my eyes away,
Yet my heart could never depart from you, the death to my soul would be the pay.
We're not perfect so I lean on God to work with our flaws, my emotions and my frustrations.
Looking too long at the offense until the fence is built between you and me, we'd meet relational devastation.
So God's Word keeps my spirit in consecration, never putting a big I before an important you.
I've been given too much grace so I face my own pride and forgive so that our intimacy can renew.
So that you could never misconstrue a moment of disappointment with a desire to leave.
I made a commitment and I meant it; my love chases after you, spending an eternity to cleave.

WHAT IS LOVE

And the world probably couldn't ever believe that I could see the worst of you yet am still amazed at your glory.
I just hope you always see it to, and if not I'm always here to remind you that your faults could never tell your story. Unless, it is to be mentioned how you overcame them, how we will never be the same since we faced what was between us just to embrace a kiss.
And for our problems, we speak victory every time we name them, how healing suddenly came when all of our charges against each other were dismissed.
So only for a moment could I ever be away,
Nothing could ever separate us. It is like love glued our heart this way, and I don't ever want that bond to fade.
I forgive you now for future faults just to save the time that is loss placing so much energy on the mistakes we've made.

CHAPTER 9:
It Keeps No Record of Wrongs

If I was to select a random group of people to tell me about the elements of their past, I'd obviously get varying stories from each of them. Some of them may speak in detail of all of their fondest of memories: family, friends, experiences in school, and vacations – nostalgically cataloguing the greatest of their experiences. Then, there would be some whose reflections would be brief, nothing of significance, nothing of importance, just a past that is just that, the past. Then, there are those who would speak in detail of the hurts and hardships, the enemies, the relationships gone bad, and the tragedies that they'd face. There are so many possibilities, but here is the reason this scenario has been brought up: it is not that the optimists do not have tragedy in their lives, they just choose to not allow those things to be the first things they recall. Here's the other thing, the tragedy-ridden people also have better events within their pasts, but they are not programmed to recall those moments. And the people in the middle... well, let's pray that they begin to consider the significance of the events of their lives.

So, in this chapter, as we move through I Corinthians 13, we come to the part of the verse that says that love keeps no record of wrongs or that it does not take into account a wrong endured. When I read this verse, the first person I thought about was Joseph in the Bible. Some of us are familiar with the story. Joseph's brothers deeply wronged him, and from that he endured many other hardships directly stemming from his brothers' actions. It was so bad that in Genesis 50:15 it says "When Joseph's brothers saw that their father was dead, they said 'What if Joseph holds a grudge against us and pays us back for all the wrongs we did to him?'" In verse nine, however, Joseph says to them, "Don't be afraid. Am I in the place of God? You intended to harm me, but God intended it for good to accomplish what is now being done, the saving of many lives."

I love scripture! It offers so much perspective. When I read Joseph's response, the first thing I asked myself and I want to now ask you is have you put yourself in the place of God in your relationship? Have you judged or condemned someone for wronging you? So often in relationships, when somebody does something wrong to someone in the relationship, that person wants to now pay them back, an eye for an eye. We begin to play a game called "Who has the biggest sword?" We get hurt and wronged and we become vindictive. Small offenses, large offenses. It doesn't matter. Part of the problem is we feel like the wrong done is a shot at our dignity, our esteem, our respect and our worth so we feel like we have to respond in a certain way to assert our dignity and respect, but is there anything to respect about retaliating? Didn't Jesus instruct us to "turn the other [cheek] towards him also [simply ignore insignificant insults or trivial losses and do not bother to retaliate—maintain your dignity, your self-respect, your poise], (Matthew 5:39)" also? In the previous chapter, we noted that it was actually honorable to overlook a wrong endured. Jesus said that if you love those who love you, what reward will you get? Unbelievers do that. He speaks more of his people choosing to do good to those that have wronged them. Jesus said to love our enemies, which is a good thing; however, some of us put more effort into doing that than we do in loving those we are supposed to have a relationship with.

And I get it. The reality is that it hurts when it is someone close to us, someone we trusted, and someone we thought loved us as we loved them. Let's take into account that Joseph was betrayed by his own brothers. They actually originally wanted him dead; they conspired to murder him. How hurtful is that? And his response is, "Am I in the place of God?" Amazing!

See, we can really learn something here. In our dealings with people, especially those we are in relationship with, we need a healthy perspective of where God stands and where we stand. This becomes difficult for two kinds of people: the self-righteous and the spoiled. What I want to tell you now is take into account all that God has forgiven you for, all that he didn't decide to pay you back for and the fact that he didn't abandon you. But here's the thing, some of us do not think our sins are really that bad. In fact, the type of sins we are guilty of are pretty "common" sins. God knows our hearts, right? "I don't sin that much," is the inner thought in our minds. Yeah right. We've simply failed to keep record of our own sin because we are keeping track of everyone else's. James 2:10 says "For whoever keeps the whole Law but stumbles in one point, he has become guilty of [breaking] all of it." However, the self-righteous find no conviction in this scripture.

And the spoiled group actually knows that they sin. They know that they couldn't afford salvation. So many times they have come close to having to pay for their sins but God was gracious. The problem with both of these groups is that there has been no guilt, no brokenness at the thought of sinning against God – the one-sided relationship. God has to do all of the loving, and he receives so little appreciation for it. Do we really take the time to fathom, "Jesus, I'd be on my way to hell without you?" "I'd be cut off from God: He wouldn't refer to me as His son. He wouldn't call me friend. I'd be forever separated from his glory." We don't think about that when someone has wronged us; we want to see them go through a little hell.

I've been wronged by someone who is supposed to love me, but am I in the place of God? We tend to deal with it better when the wrong experienced was an accident, but Joseph's brothers committed pre-meditated wrongs. So, men, your wife may intentionally be withholding sex. She's ignoring your calls on purpose. She's slandering your name to friends and family. Women, he's neglecting duties around the house so that you'd eventually do it. He's avoiding disciplining the children. He stared at that other woman a little too long.

> The enemy wanted our wrongs to overtake us.

Though a concern remains a concern, the objective does not involve retaliation.

Joseph said, "What you meant for my harm, God meant for my good." "God meant for it to accomplish what is being done right now, the saving of many lives." Before my wife and I got married, we prayed and sought God. We were seeking spiritual discernment to know if it was actually meant for us to get married. Both of us had had previous relationships. We'd been "in-love" in previous relationships. We wanted to lean on something more. Of course, we got our answer and moved forward. Even though we sought God, neither one of us could've ever known or anticipated some of the misfortune we would bring to one another. I'm sure there are many other married people who can relate. You sit back and you ask God, "You sure we're supposed to be together?" "I don't think love and marriage are supposed to be like this." "Look how she does me." "Look at how he does me." "This is not working right now."

Let me be honest with you. The enemy wanted our wrongs to overtake us; yet, God has been using our wrongs to shape us. The hell in my marriage has been shaping me. Nights that felt like death have resurrected me. When you can feel like you have nothing left to give and wake up to discover you have so much more stored up, there is a spiritual strength that wakes up inside of you. This strength comes with facing, in love, in hope, and in truth, the wrongs committed towards you. It is glorious to, in word and deed, communicate that there is nothing that can make you stop loving the one who are with. I cannot express in words the fulfillment of her communicating, "Despite everything, you're still the man for me." See, that doesn't mean anything or respectfully not that much until you have been through some things. Like many things, it is easier said than done. However, you don't have to intentionally look for trouble. Just try to live this thing out God's way and trouble will find you.

Jesus figured it out. While being persecuted, while dying on a cross, He said "Forgive them for they know not what they do." Jesus literally had to go through hell to be exalted as Lord and Savior. He went and got the keys. He took all of death's power and saved souls in the process. He chose not to focus on the wrong endured so he could have strength for His mission.

Isn't it a great feeling to know that He knew all the wrong you'd do, even after you chose to follow Him, yet He still fashioned you before you were even in the womb, purposed you, and committed all of His love for you? In the presence of people, mainly those in relationships, He's not asking us to do anything He hasn't already liberally and abundantly done for us. We have the opportunities to extend the same love, grace and peace to the people that is supposed to matter to us the most. If our own mates aren't important enough, who will be?

Sometimes our mates do things intentionally to harm us, but God has great intentions in your process. To be real with you, I wouldn't have written this book if it were not for some of the wrongs experienced. Especially for the people that desire healthy relationships, wrongs have a way of making it evident that we are works in progress and that we need God at work to progress us.

So far, we have only covered how we correspond to wrongs and not fully the idea of keeping records of wrongs. There are, in fact, dangers in doing that. Of course, recording means to write down, document and/or track something. Records are peculiar things.

Think about it. Someone with a felony can tell you how detrimental a bad record can be to someone. A snapshot of their lives dictates their livelihood – one major offense. Jobs, relationships and well-being all challenged by having a record. We stop seeing the person; we only see the "felon" – the bad person. Sadly enough, we treat others even better, even though they may have done similar or worse things, but there is just simply no record of it. Job applications do not ask if you have ever committed a felony; they only ask if you have been convicted of committing one – if there is a record of it.

Likewise in our relationships, when we have the mindset to document and keep track of wrongs, we begin to label our counterparts. We assign negative connotations to them because of their faults. We withdraw trust, love and admiration. We begin to devalue them. And trust me, when we do this, they pick up on it, too. How can you expect to give your all in a relationship when you're keeping track of all the wrongs you've endured? It is virtually impossible. Just as it is with our law system, it doesn't take a bunch of wrongs, just let one big wrong happen to us and our mates will have to pay for it for the rest of their lives all because we wanted to document it. What happens is that, when we document it, we want to reference it every time we can use it to make an argument. Whether it happened last week, a year ago, or ten years ago, we want it to be relevant in every circumstance. In order to love properly we have to forget about these wrongs and move on.

God, our Creator, understands this. Even He has to practice the art and skill of not accounting our wrongs in order to continue to be good to us.

I, only I, am He who wipes out your transgressions for my own sake, and I will not remember your sins. Remind me [of your merits with a thorough report], let us plead and argue our case together; state your position, that you may be proved right. ~Isaiah 43:25

Now, I don't know if you've ever thought about how profound this verse is. We all believe God to be all-knowing, yet if he has not remembered our sins, is He truly all-knowing? I believe the answer is "Yes, He is all-knowing," and I'm delighted to explain how.

Dismember means to take apart. If you dismember a band, it means that the members of the band are no longer together. They are no longer a unit. So in contrast, to remember is to put the parts of something back together again.

As far as the east is from the west, so far has He removed our transgressions from us. ~Psalms 103:12

God has dismembered us from our sin, which is essentially our wrongs committed against Him. He will not remember them or reattach them to us. He knows about them, but he will not associate them any longer as a part of us. It is also profound that both of these scriptures are in the Old Testament, long before he sent Jesus to separate us from our sinful ways once and for all. God loved us so that, in His mind, He chose not to see us in our sin but to see us in His overwhelming pursuit for us.

Do not remember the wrongs of our loved ones. We must spiritually grow and learn how to dismember them from their faults. The truth is that they can actually be removed from the roots of what drives those wrongs against us. But if we keep them together in our minds, we will never be driven by the redemptive spirit of love. Jesus sacrificed Himself to atone and pay for our sins so that we wouldn't. Trust that there is enough grace in your account to offer it to your mate. I'll interject here and remind you that there is nothing wrong with discussing or communicating hurts or wrongs, but do it from a place of desiring reconciliation, not to antagonize them for their faults.

In business, there is a saying, "You get what you measure." You need more revenue? Measure it. You need market share? Measure it. You need more margin? You got it. Measure it. Likewise, if you are keeping tabs on wrongs, your relationship is certain to look more wrong than it will look right. You're looking for wrong, so you'll find wrong. It is the way the brain works.

As a young boy, I remember waiting to get picked up by my parents from school. Let's just say that the family car was red at that time. Well, as I waited, I saw so many red cars. I even thought to myself, "Why are there so many red cars on the road today?" The reality is that there are probably that many red cars on the road on any day. The true difference was that I was looking for the red car, so I noticed more of them. I was anticipating it, so I noticed everything that looked like my parents' car, even though, obviously, they weren't my parents.

In our relationships, we experience a wrong and we anticipate a pattern. We begin to notice more wrongs, and we begin to even perceive things as being wrong that really aren't wrong, all because we are keeping track of them. And here's the thing. There could have been just as many blue cars or black cars on the road at the time that I was looking for my parents' red car, but I wouldn't have known because I wasn't looking for a black or a blue car. In the same token, there could be a lot more going well in our relationships, but we wouldn't know because we are no longer looking for the good in our relationships and in our significant others. We are too busy keeping records of wrongs, and as we start doing that, it is a slippery slope in our relationships.

You know what I like? Photo albums. Nobody really ever takes the time to capture negative moments, print them and place them inside of photo albums. Bad pictures rarely ever make the album, and the ones that do offer some special sense of value that perhaps can only be shared by the people in the picture and by the one who captured it all. Like a picture of a baby crying, of course the baby was unhappy in the moment, but, to the mother, it reminds her of the delicate stage of her beloved child. Of course there are some bad times and sorrow in between the pictures, but we don't keep a record of it. We are careful to draw out the value in those moments and allow them to outweigh those not-so-good moments.

So, in our relationships, build a "photo book," not a case file. Photo books highlight all the qualities in our relationships. They foster love and appreciation. When we put our past together or remember it, we leave the sour parts out, and we do not give account to the pain endured but to the trial overcome by love. We recognize our growth over the years and we appreciate our story. But when we build case files, we introduce criticisms and judgment, arguments and strife, and we drive each other away. We ignore the positives in order to prove the other guilty of crimes. With one act, we believe it is enough evidence to condemn them for life. We have zero remorse. We are driven and dictated by hurt, resentment and pride. We see our relationships from a you-and-me standpoint and rarely from an "us" standpoint. We fail to exercise any level of grace, failing to acknowledge the abundance of grace God offers us daily.

Forgiveness is a true gateway to releasing loved ones from the record of offenses. Forgiveness cannot be earned by the person who needs to be forgiven, no more than we can earn God's forgiveness. It is a gift. However, for some of us, it is not a gift we are eager to give. Some of us feel like they "win" if we just let them off of the hook. Some of us, honestly, want them to suffer more to the measure or greater than what we suffered. Pride and ego drive some of us to hold the grudges that we hold against our loved ones. In it, we allow this unforgiveness to keep us separate. Many of us have heard the saying that unforgiveness is like drinking poison and expecting the other person to suffer. It is true; forgiveness offers us healing as well as the person we are forgiving. Our flesh stubbornly holds on anyway. I mean, our flesh is condemned already. It might as well wreak havoc on our souls and spirits while it still has the opportunity, and because we believe it is protecting us or offering something of value, we continue to allow it. I cannot express how spiritually irresponsible and immature this is. We have to grow up.

In defense of our human nature, I admit that it can be hard to forgive. Sometimes, even when we desire to, it seems like the very thought of it causes hurt and suffering. We rather just leave the unforgiveness there and try to move on with life. When I was a teenager, one day I played basketball at my neighbor's house. The basketball goal was located in his yard. The ground was predominantly dirt so you could still manage to bounce the ball effectively. For whatever reason, I thought it was okay to play in some sandals with some white tube socks on. My socks became dirtier by the minute, but we didn't care. We played a very intense game of basketball. During the game, suddenly, I took a step and felt a sharp pain in my toe. I thought I had stepped on a nail. However, when I looked at my foot, I didn't see anything, so I continued to play.

After the game was over, I examined my foot again to notice that the bottom of my sock was covered with blood. Perplexed, I checked closely again only to find no reason for all of the blood. Later that evening, I retired at another friend's house. I was spending the night over. During my shower, I stepped on that same toe and felt something different. I looked at my foot and noticed a glass shard sticking out from my toe. It had been lodged into my toe that entire time. It was so sensitive to the touch. As long as I didn't touch it, I didn't feel any pain, but the moment I felt the slightest touch, it was agonizing.

To avoid the pain, I attempted to sleep that night with the shard still in my foot. I thought it might fall out on its own. It was cold that night, but I could not use a blanket because it was heavy enough to cause my toe a considerable amount of pain and discomfort, so I attempted to use a bed sheet as I laid on his floor. In the freezing cold of the night, the slightest movement under the sheet caused enough pain to keep me awake. Finally, in the middle of the night, frustrated, I got up and returned to my friend's bathroom.

There, I sat on the bathroom counter. I literally prayed to God. I told Him that I needed His help to remove this glass from my toe. It is painful and I just want peace and rest for the night. After I prayed, I grabbed my ankle as tightly as I could with one hand and I reached for the glass with the other and pulled. It came out so easily and painless. Yes, touching it was painful, but pulling it out was nothing. I immediately considered all of the time I had wasted and endured by letting it remain in my foot. I was free from the glass shard and my foot could begin to heal.

This is our situation with hurt. To think about forgiving will be painful. We will consider all of the reasons why we shouldn't. We have to relive the situation every time we consider it. It will not allow us to have any peace or to truly rest. If we would pray to God and ask Him to help us forgive, we can muster up the strength to just do it. Once we do, the pain will go away and we can finally begin the process of healing.

Love keeps no records of wrongs. As far as the east is from the west, love separates the sins from those who has His love. As I learn that my love is equipped to cover your sin, in essence, your wrong is doing a good work in me, because I'm spiritually maturing and my love isn't fleeing from you but, in fact, growing towards you. Eagerly, my love is now desiring to remind you of who you are. You are God's child. You are His precious gift to me: the object of my affection and intimacy. You are my love and my heart, and I do not have to and do not desire to define you by anything else!

So You Can Stay

When I think of us, the only thing I want to reflect on is the good times. It's a love crime to present any material that says that we shouldn't be.
Surely there will be bad things that happen but they don't define us. The process of overcoming them refines us, shaping the better you and a better me.
If we could see our past and our future simultaneously, we'd be convinced that there's no need to hold on to hurt.

WHAT IS LOVE

Our relationship is a great production. God is the writer and director, our protector from destruction as long as we continue to put Him first.
Some focus on the pain, I focus on the power.
Holding a grudge against you is like holding my breath; it's impossible to do that for an hour.
I got to get back to loving you.
And remembering who you are to me reminds me of what I'm supposed to do.
That's why it's important not to cloud that picture which your mistakes.
To say that you're not worth my love anymore is the lie that it creates.
Resentment builds a wall and hate within permeates.
It is such an undesirable equation that calculates up to heartbreaks.
So when I think of you and I think of us, I ignore all of the fuss, the fighting, and anything else that will cause my love to stray.
Because at the end of the day, the last thing I want to be is just a memory. I want you right here next to me, so I send my hurt away so you can stay.

CHAPTER 10:
Love Does Not Delight in Evil but Rejoices with the Truth

    Two friends are both invited to an evening engagement. They both eagerly accept in anticipation of a great evening. The host directly tells them to save their appetites because the chef would be preparing the food and personally serving them. Both, enthused and feeling honored, refrained from consuming anything before arriving. They dress in their best evening outfits and walk into an amazing ambiance. The music is live, full of instruments and melodic singing. And just as promised, the chef delivers: Porter steaks, baked chicken, shrimp, salmon, duck... Entre after entre, it seems like the chef prepared every main dish imaginable.

    One of the friends was excited to the point that he almost couldn't contain himself. He didn't know where to start with having so many options, but he knew that he wanted to sample as much as possible. He

WHAT IS LOVE

turned to the other friend to notice that he looked full of disappointment. It seemed all of the splendor of the moment had went away. What could have possibly happened to cause him to look upon the evening in disgust? It turns out that he had become a vegan and, amongst all of the food that was presented, there was not a single dish prepared without meat or the use of an ingredient created by an animal. He knew none of the prepared dishes would sit well in his system. His digestive system had become conformed to the lifestyle of consuming fresh vegetables and fruits. All of the food prepared satisfied one friend but not the other.

I Corinthians 13 teaches us that love doesn't delight in evil but rejoices with the truth.

For the sinful nature has its desire which is opposed to the Spirit, and the desire of the Spirit opposes the sinful nature; for these [two, the sinful nature and the Spirit] are in direct opposition to the other [continually in conflict], so that you [as believers] do not [always] do whatever [good things] you want to do. ~ Galatians 5:17

In the same manner, it is something very different than love that is pleased in evil things. The thing is, we are all wrapped in flesh, and all of our flesh (yes, mine and yours) desire to do evil things and further delights in them.

For I know that nothing good lives in me, that is, in my flesh [my human nature, my worldiness – my sinful capacity]. ~ Romans 7:18

As Paul admitted, our flesh doesn't desire to and does not produce anything good – and this is our human nature, which means natural. It is natural to desire to do things that are worldly or sinful. It doesn't have to be taught. This means that what is natural will not seem wrong but simply as a part of us, but our spirits are able to see them as wrong. But if our spirits aren't governing us, then how can we recognize the wrong? Without the spirit, we cannot love. Without the spirit, we delight in evil.

The way of fools seem right to them... ~ Proverbs 12:15

Most of us have justified our ways and character, but they are actually killing us: our souls, our spirits, our relationships and our bodies.

There is a way that appears to be right, but in the end it leads to death. ~ Proverbs 14:12

I believe we do so much evil with a perspective that makes it seem justified or with good motives but we are actually killing our relationships in the process.

My assumption for some of us out there is that we believe we are not "delighting in evil." "Come on, BJ, evil is a strong word." "I know I am not perfect, but I don't do anything that is evil." We can euphemize our actions as long as we want to but the truth is the truth, sin is sin, and evil is evil. As a society, we split hairs and say it is a little sin, or that something is bad but not evil. The dictionary, however, simply says that evil is something morally wrong or bad, harmful; injurious. That means that we do not have to sacrifice goat's blood or practice witchcraft to commit an evil act. Lying to someone is evil. Disrespecting someone is an evil act. Verbal abuse is evil. The sooner we accept the extremity of it, hopefully, the sooner we will be uncomfortable committing evil acts. We will more sincerely turn away from them moving forward.

There can possibly be some things in ourselves and exampled in our relationships that are actually evil but remain natural in our perspectives. They are so closely tied to us that we dismiss it as part of our personality, our culture and/or our society. They are so natural that we are unbothered when they surface. In fact, some of us use evil acts as coping mechanisms, as defense, for power and respect sake, and for control. We are so married to the evil acts that we tell our mates, "This is me, so deal with it." Not sure what I'm talking about? I am speaking of jealousy, stubbornness, fits of rage, and lust. You ever find comfort or delight in being stubborn in an argument? You selfishly didn't want them to have their way or "win the argument" so you stubbornly disagreed, stubbornly ignored what was important because you found delight in not having to be wrong or feel like a failure. That sounds like delighting in evil to me.

Has jealousy and insecurity ever driven you to demand that they call you every hour or respond to your text messages within minutes? Maybe they cannot hang out with others without you because you don't want somebody else to try to talk to them. If somebody else smiles at them, it is a problem. They cannot have friends of the opposite sex. You have to be their only source of happiness. Jealousy helps you set up boundaries to avoid your fear of being left or misused. You delight in the fact that your actions, driven by jealousy, make you feel safe. Sounds like delighting in evil to me.

During arguments, you are so "passionate" (I've been so guilty of this one). You get loud to stress your point. You choose words to cut deep to place them under you, to establish some power, independence and confidence. You find a need to put them in their place so you don't feel out of place. Your sense of feeling appreciated or your esteem is so challenged that you become overbearing as a defense. You lack the method of being vulnerable in communication so fits of rage help you hide your weakness in this mirage of power and authority. This sounds like delighting in evil to me.

Again, we prefer not to use this four-letter word because as long as we don't, we don't receive the pressure to let it go. We selfishly want to keep some of the evil. We trust more in these evil weapons than we trust in God's ways. God's ways become good for our image but not as important to our character. It is like claiming God has given us peace yet we are killing ourselves with downers every night in order to be able to go to sleep. We aren't being genuine or authentic. Love makes the choice to overthrow evil ways. Like a vegan in a meat market, nothing is satisfying about it.

Have you realized you may be guilty of delighting in evil yet? I have and I'm relying on God to help me do something about it. But just in case you haven't, let's explore another situation where we may find ourselves guilty of this evil. You know it is said that money is amoral. It is not good or evil. The Bible says that the love of money is evil. Also, how someone intends to use the money determines if it is an evil or a good use. Feeding the poor - good use. Bribing a judge - bad use. Likewise, sometimes we can solicit amoral or seemingly good acts from our mates but they serve an evil agenda.

Some of us solicit compliments from our mates on a regular basis. We want them to be into us and make us feel like kings and queens. Again, nothing really seems wrong on the surface. However, sometimes, if we

WHAT IS LOVE

look a little deeper, we'll notice that we are seeking flattery to appeal to our ego or pride. We really care less about how it lets us know how they feel about us and more so how it helps us feel better about ourselves. The danger is that it produces a parasitic and not an intimate connection. Because it is more about how it makes us feel about ourselves and not about how it makes us feel about our union, the flattery is almost if not actually equally appealing if received from someone else. You can't tell me that it is not delighting in evil. We are feeding the flesh. Men are not the only ones guilty of this next one. We use our mates' bodies to fulfill our lust, our bodily needs. We love that scripture too:

Do not deprive each other except perhaps by mutual consent and for a time, so that you may devote yourselves to prayer. Then come together again so that Satan will not tempt you because of your lack of self-control.
~ I Corinthians 7:5

Now, whereas sex is a marital right, this scripture is not a ticket to fulfill your lust craves. And I'll say that, husbands, if you have not established intimacy between you and your wife, you have deprived her more of marital rights than however many times she's said no to you in bed. Though sex is a marital right, it still is evil to use it to fill fleshly desires. Are you not sure if you are being driven by the flesh or the spirit? Pay attention to your thoughts in your pursuit. Does your pursuit have anything to do with her or your union or is it strictly based on your bodily needs, desires and passions? If you disconnect with her right after the moment of release, that's lust, Buddy.

Some other amoral examples are that of gifts or other things money can buy. Are you desiring memories, meaningful treasures or is it greed or materialism that drives you? Nothing is wrong with a man or a woman pampering their mates. However, similar to the sex situation, if you find yourself more connected to the object or experience than you are to your mate afterwards, that is selfish, materialistic and evil. It may hurt to hear it, but it is the truth. The material part of the experience should not receive the greater praise and appreciation. This is a common one, unfortunately, that we are found guilty. We praised the food and don't consider the chef. And to avoid a long list, we magnify the blessings and not the blesser. In our relationships, we desire all the love we can get and materialize our lovers.

But it feels good, doesn't it? We feel so good feeding the flesh. It is not of God to be this way, even for the things we need.

For the [pagan] eagerly seeks all these things; [but do not worry,] for your heavenly Father knows that you need them. But first and most importantly seek (aim at, strive after) His kingdom and His righteousness [His way of doing and being right-the attitude and character of God], and all these things will be given to you also.
~Matthew 6:32-33

We must prioritize our pursuits and developing the proper character with God is top of the list. Selfishly seeking to fulfill self at the expense of others is not God's way; it is evil.

Now, the last area of delighting in evil that I want to cover, as it pertains to relationships, is that of feeling happy when something bad, evil or harmful happens to our mates, even if they did something wrong. "He got in an accident? That's what he gets. He shouldn't have went out last night while I was here by myself with the baby." "She didn't make it to the interview on time? That's what she gets. She shouldn't have been worrying about what I was doing and just took care of her own business." "Ha! Nobody came to his show? That's his fault for walking around like he's all that." Man, we can be so ugly to one another. What does that say about us when we rejoice or delight in the hurts or downfalls of our mates? Of anyone, actually?

> **Discipline and punishment are not synonymous.**

See that no one repays another with evil for evil, but always seeks that which is good for one another and for all people. ~I Thessalonians 5:15

Whether by our hands or not, it is evil to delight in evil being done to anybody. We definitely shouldn't want it to happen to someone we love or have an interest in. When they hurt us, we shouldn't be overjoyed or fulfilled in "paying them back." Love doesn't desire to do that. There is a difference between desiring correction and merely desiring punishment. Now, punishment may be a tool of discipline but not the goal. Discipline desires that someone learns from the consequences to become better and draw closer to their potential, so that we can walk healthier together. Punishment is more concerned with someone learning not to hurt, offend, or wrong me anymore, otherwise I anticipate them paying more for their choices in the future. We often choose punishment not to rectify problems but to emphasize hurt or disappointment. We must mature in our relationships. If punishment is used as a tool, let it be part of the ultimate goal of reconciliation.

I may need some time away because I was offended, but I still desire to come back to you with forgiveness and the open communication to resolve the problem. We may have to cancel a date because you didn't take care of your part of the plans, but I'll give us a chance in the future to do a better job of planning and implementation. Remember this, even when our mates sin, it is never a time to rejoice in the punishment. It is a time for sorrow over the sin. Still, remember we are to seek the good in one another.

So we have covered the love "does not delight in evil" part, and now it is time to cover the "rejoices with the truth" part. Simply put, love, delights in God's laws and ways, desiring to both learn and follow them.

If you really love Me, you will keep my commandments.
~ John 14:15

For the [true] love of God is this: that we habitually keep His commandments and remain focused on His precepts.
~ I John 5:3

And here's the thing, it may not be natural to do so, but it is not difficult. We just have to genuinely

WHAT IS LOVE

desire to do so, and that perhaps is a process. I John goes on to say:

And His precepts are not difficult [to obey]. For everyone born of God is victorious and overcomes the world; and this is that victory that has conquered and overcome the world - our [continuing, persistent] faith [in Jesus the Son of God].

It's no surprise that in John 14:6 Jesus informed that He was the Way, the Truth and the Life. Remember, spiritual things such as genuine, powerful, soul saving, relationship molding love cannot operate out of human nature and its worldliness. That is why love delights in following God's ways and laws and not the world's ways. It cannot function properly within human nature.

Let your spirit love because God says love. Forgive because God says forgive. Be kind because God says be kind. Don't lie because God instructs us not to lie. Be faithful because God says be faithful. Submit because God says submit. Be patient because God says be patient.

Now, if you cringed at any of those things, it isn't love that is making you do so, it is your flesh. Those things do not feel good to our flesh. Our flesh doesn't delight in them. Remember, it desires what is contrary to the Spirit. It desires what is contrary to love. Love turns towards God's ways in fear, awe, reverence, and trust. Now, of course, we are not perfect, but when we disobey these things, love does not spend time to justify it. "I lied so that I wouldn't hurt her feelings." "I cheated because my needs weren't getting met." "I don't submit because I don't feel like he is doing a good job being the pastor of our home." Again, love does not delight or justify turning away from God's commands. Love corrects and turns back to them. Love approaches these situations within the boundaries of God's commands. Love says, "Let me ask the spirit to help me deliver difficult information to her in the way she can receive it without being offended." Love says, "I'm feeling a void, but I'm trusting God to fulfill my relationship." Love says, "Lord, help me honor and respect him as the Godly man you've called him to be. I know and have faith that he will arrive to his potential." Love overcomes. Love, by the power of God, experiences victory!

Along with God's laws and ways, all of his words stand as the truth - a truth that we can rejoice in, even in our relationships.

So will My word be which goes out of My mouth; it will not return to Me void (useless, without result). Without accomplishing what I desire, and without succeeding in the matter of for which I sent it. ~Isaiah 55:11

I believe it is important in our relationships to have some truths of God to stand on. I want to share with you a few of my own, but I encourage you to take note of your own to carry you through difficult or uncertain seasons.

Many are the afflictions of the righteous, but God delivers them from them all. ~ Psalms 34:19

I take note that my relationship will experience afflictions, but by trusting God, we will surely witness his deliverance.

For his anger is but for a moment, his favor is for lifetime. Weeping may endure for a night but joy comes in the morning. ~Psalms 30:5

We will make mistakes; however, God is only temporarily disappointed. His great desires for us are far more eternal, so should ours be for each other. Our mistakes may bring sorrow for a moment, but God zealously shines his light on us by day. By day, let our lights shine for each other.

Above all, have fervent and unfailing love for one another, because love covers a multitude of sins. ~ I Peter 4:8

I realize that we will sin against one another, multiple times in our lifetime, love is effective in covering them all. Don't waste time on complaining about what love was intended to do.

He who finds a wife, finds a good thing and obtains favor and approval from the Lord. ~ Proverbs 18:22

No matter what I may perceive as imperfect or negative, my wife is my good thing. With her, God offers me favor and approval. Let me honor what my God has deemed good.

Above all, let's mature. Our human nature does not have to govern our character. Like someone going vegan or changing their diet, the new food may seem foreign and perhaps not delightful, but that is only because we are so used to some poor eating choices. Over time, we would not even desire the old food habits, and if we were to ever abruptly turn back, we'd be sick. Likewise, too many evil or ungodly practices may be a regular practice right now. It may be seemingly distasteful to pursue our relationships God's way. But when we become habitual in our obedience, worldly ways will no longer sit well in us because the spirit will reign. This is what will allow love to operate at an optimum level. God's words, ways, laws and promises are there for us, and they are the truths for our spirits. Let's trust Him enough to see the glory of God revealed in our lives and inside of our relationships.

Even When

I would never enjoy seeing you in pain or hurt. You should think again if at first you ever thought I'd possess such an ill desire towards you.
Seeing life hit you hard is an indirect abuse to me. How can we walk together as one if I'm not sensitive to the things you go through?
So, especially in times I feel helpless to you, I hold on to the truth.
Even when the solution is not in my hands, at the end of the day, I know God continues to hold you.
In everything we face it is God's face that moves with haste to sort out all our matters.
Even when we do not possess answers to all of our problems, the fact that God can solve them is all that matters.
Even when it is hard to move forward, God's word can give us the strength to stand.
When we don't understand, we still can trust and obey His command.
Even when you've done something to hurt me, I'd rather bear it than let it break the bond we share.
I leave it to God to move heaven and earth keep us together, through seasons and weather, I know that He cares.
So I'll never choose vengeance or to be vindictive, though you slay me yet I will trust.

God's Word is all the power we need to overcome even our darkest hour so keeping faith in Him is a must.

CHAPTER 11:
Love Always Protects

You know, sometimes I wonder if I'm being a bit dramatic with my efforts to talk about love, marriage, and intimacy in relationships. I, self-consciously at times, think people think it is not that important. I could be wrong in my concern. At this point, no critic has approached me and said, "Chill out, it is not that serious." On the other hand, I wonder if people will read these revelations and simply think, "oh, that's nice" but won't stress any urgency or intent to passionately pursue a stronger, wiser mindset when it comes to dating and walking out a life in marriage.

Allow me to point something out just in case you haven't noted it. There is perhaps a consensus that the number one enemy to God and man is Satan. When did he show up to man? God breathed into Adam and created him in his own image. No Satan. He gave him dominion over all of the land, over every sea creature and land animal - still no Satan. God puts Adam to sleep and creates Eve from his rib under the thought, "it is not good for man to be alone." All of a sudden, Satan shows up.

I believe there is a reason he shows up now, well a few reasons. First and foremost, with Eve present, God, Adam and Eve now have an opportunity to establish a new spiritual legacy in the offspring that would now be created. Can you imagine a world full of millions and millions of people, unblemished, perfect spirits, walking in the image of God? No sin. It's difficult to picture, perhaps, but it was God's intentions, the very intentions Satan wanted to destroy.

Another reason Satan attacks at this moment, is because there is now a greater opportunity to create division. As much as Adam trusted God, he also loved his wife Eve, he currently had no reason not to trust her as well. By inserting a little doubt and curiosity into Eve, Adam would have to choose, and we all know how that story ended.

Lastly, God had given Adam a lot of instructions on what to do, but now we see, for the first time, God given Adam instructions on what not to do: eat of the forbidden fruit. Curiosity is funny. If I told you not to look up right now, even if you had not desired to before, now there is a curiosity if not desire to now look up. Adam had not been denied anything up until this point. As it forever remains in humankind, temptation was born, and Satan would use it against Adam and Eve.

Nonetheless, for the same reasons he attacked Adam and Eve, Satan attacks our hearts and our relationships, especially our marriages. He wants to eliminate the chances of spiritual legacy. In marriage, God instructs us to love each other as He loved the church. Satan doesn't want that. God saw an imperfect church, loved it unconditionally, and still trusts the institution to give birth to new members of the Christian body. Together, they work to raise these babes in Christ. In the same likeness, the man, unconditionally loves his wife, despite imperfections, trusts her to birth his children, and they work together to raise them to be children of God.

In I Timothy 3:5, it is asked, *"If anyone does not know how to manage his own family, how can he take care of God's church?"* This scripture is in reference to qualifications of overseers and deacons. On the same note, we see that the roles and purposes are first to be exemplified in the home. Thus, the home is considered to be a man's first church. A child's relationship with God or lack thereof is mostly predicated on the home life.

For that reason, Satan desires to destroy the fabric of family, and he has found that the most effective way to do that is to destroy the institution of marriage. It has been proven that children suffer from absentee fathers. It has been proven that children take years to recover from divorce. Has been proven that children tend to emotionally, mentally and spiritually suffer in dysfunctional homes. Children, who grow up in single-parent homes, struggle without seeing the roles of husband and wife modeled in the home, so they struggle in their relationships. If Satan destroys the roots, the fruit will die, so he attacks every family tree.

John 10:10 says that the thief comes to "steal, kill and destroy." In marriages, we see the devil stealing time away through strife birthed out of our pride, jealousy, rudeness and unforgiveness. He kills intimacy with our lust, our envy, our debauchery, and our unlovingness. With his consistent attacks and his unrelenting pursuits, he destroys not only marriages, but generations. There should be no question about it. Satan is God's and love's public enemy number one.

The world is also an enemy of love. In every aspect, the world represents rebellion towards God. In all efforts, the world aims to have everything that God promises without following his ways and directions to receive them. God desires communion with man, the world desires enslavement, to use man to fulfill its selfish and lustful desires.

Love stands in the way of that. The world doesn't want you acquainted with Godly love because it couldn't get you to succumb to its tactics of enslavement. Basically, love is fulfilling. That is to say to love and be loved is fulfilling. The world creates its power by creating and deepening the voids in our spirits, identities and relationships. The world creates these voids by feeding our flesh, our sinful ways and their unending appetites.

Think about it. Are you paying attention? If you turn on the news, stream social media, or any other media source, you see a host of negativity: crime, murder, racism, child neglect, trafficking, rape, abuse, and celebrity divorces and relationship scandals. The world wants you to know how negative it desires to portray itself. Why? Depressed people fuel the economy. They buy things to make themselves happy. They buy drugs and alcohol to escape the pressures of life. Scared people fuel the economy. They buy weapons, security, and take self-defense classes.

The world also promotes insecurities and vanity. It is now difficult not to compare yourself to somebody else. We post pictures and statements for likes on social media. Grown men and women, zealously follow every trend to be in-the-know and to be one of the popular kids in school, again. Both women and men spend money on plastic surgeries, enhancements, clothes, supplements, gym memberships, and not at all to be healthier but either to avoid being the ugly person or to promote a sense of vanity and boasting.

The reality is that with love, we are strong enough to overcome all of these things. Yes, mayhem is going on in the world, but love offers a sense of strength and courage to fulfill each day - to overcome hatred, racism, sexism and any other thing that prevents us from walking together. Love understands that everybody has value and should be honored, whether you are skinny, fat, short, tall, young, old, rich or poor. Love doesn't suggest you escape reality but acknowledge who you are - the apple of God's eye. We'd still exercise; not to compete with each other's looks or to feel sexy, but to take care of God's temple. Love allows us to live out our days with triumphant joy so we'd never overstretch our means for materialistic things. We wouldn't neglect children to be on the scene all the time. We wouldn't lay in bed with strangers to feel desired. We wouldn't put a fellow man down just to feel some false sense of power and respect.

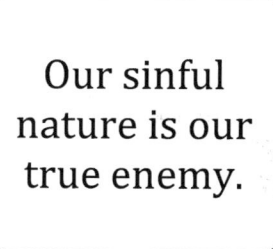

Our sinful nature is our true enemy.

Love could really heal the world, whether the world wanted it to or not. But since the world has its agenda, it points out areas where love has seemingly failed. It tries its best to convince us that we can live without love or that love doesn't truly exists. It mocks love, scoffs at anyone who claims to love or be loved, just anticipating his/her fall or demise.

A friend of mine told me about a woman that approached him in interest. He responded by telling her

WHAT IS LOVE

that he was married. She replied and told him his marriage was his problem, not hers. She had no respect for love or the institution of marriage. "Side chicks" laugh at "main chicks" for believing that their men are faithful yet overlooking the fact that they dishonor themselves. Strippers have a huge following because society now says it is okay because some of them make a lot of money. The world has taken calculated steps to phase love out of the picture, because love doesn't fuel spending. Love does not create social slaves.

And yet, there is another enemy of love. We war with it every day. It simply despises everything love stands for. It is almost impossible to ignore its voice. Right at the moments we desire to do the right thing, it speaks.

I do not understand what I do. For what I want to do I do not do, but what I hate to do. And if I do what I do not want to do, I agree that the law is good. As it is, it is no longer I myself who do it, but it is sin living in me. For I know that good itself does not dwell in me, that is my sinful nature. For I have the desire to do what is good, but I cannot carry it out. For I do not do the good I want to do, but the evil I do not want to do - this I keep on doing.
~ Romans 7:15-19

Our sinful nature is a true enemy. And as long as we live on this side, we will never escape it. It is in constant battle with love and overall with our spirits. Our sinful nature desires dominion over our souls and over our minds, to use it to carry out all of its vices and to feed its unending appetite.

For the flesh desires what is contrary to the spirit, and the spirit what is contrary to the flesh. They are in conflict

with each other, that you are not to do whatever you want.
~ Galatians 5:17

Indeed, the conflict is carried out over the span of our entire life. The spirit chooses to be humble; the flesh chooses to be prideful. The spirit desires to be forgiving; the flesh desires to harbor malice. The spirit desires genuine intimacy; the flesh desires self-fulfillment. The spirit desires to honor God; the flesh desires to honor self. Everything that the spirit stands for, the flesh desires to dismantle and destroy. What kind of war is that when the villain is yourself?

Love understands this - everything that it stands for, everything that it values, and who it values is always under attack by Satan, by the world and by our sinful natures. Because it understands that it is always under attack, love always protects.

Love protects two things: its character or reputation and the people or recipient of its love. Now, there are multiple ways to protect those things. The first method of protection is that of attacking the enemy, whether in response to the enemy's advance or in proactive pursuit to thwart the enemy's ability. In attack mode, love goes after the enemy. What is our weapon of choice?

The weapons we fight with or not the weapons of the world. On the contrary, they have divine power to demolish strongholds. ~ 2 Corinthians 10:4

So we are not attacking with guns or fists. Ephesians 6:17 tells us to:

Take the helmet of salvation and the sword of the Spirit, which is the word of God.

And Hebrews 4:12 says:

The Word of God is alive and active. Sharper than any double-edged sword, it penetrates even to dividing soul and spirit, joints and marrow; it judges the thoughts and attitudes of the heart.

So in Ephesians, it talks about how the Word of God is used to battle the devil and evil forces. And in Hebrews, it talks about how the Word of God attacks ourselves, separating soul from spirit and from flesh, revealing the attitude of the heart. The Word attacks all three enemies. But if we have no Word in us, we have no sword. We have no weapon to attack the enemies.

Take a little journey with me. First, one may argue that the Word must be heard.

Consequently, faith comes from hearing the message, and the message is heard through the word about Christ.
~ Romans 10:17

This would indicate that there is some relationship between faith, hearing and the Word. But if we read a little further, verse 18 says:

But I ask: did they not hear? Of course they did: yet the good news was not accepted by all who heard.

Therefore, hearing must not be adequate enough to "wield the sword." In other references, we see Jesus speak the word and use it as a weapon. After He fasted for 40 days and was tempted by the devil, he used the

Word of God. We see in another example how he spoke to legions of demons and caused them to jump into the bodies of pigs and cast themselves off a cliff. So maybe the power is in the speaking of the Word. However, let's take a look at Acts 19:13-16:

Some Jews who went around driving out evil spirits tried to invoke the name of the Lord Jesus over those who were demon possessed. They would say "in the name of Jesus whom Paul preaches, I command you to come out." Seven sons of Sceva, a Jewish priest, were doing this. One day the evil spirit answered them, "Jesus I know, and Paul I know about, but who are you?" Then the man who had the evil spirit jumped on them and overpowered them all. He gave them such a beating that they ran out of the house naked and bleeding.

These sons of a priest called on the name of Jesus and literally had their butts handed back to them. But they spoke his name; there is power in the name, right? But if you notice from the Scripture, they had no personal relationship with Jesus. They said "in the name of Jesus whom Paul preaches." They attempted to name drop and was unsuccessful. If we go back to Ephesians 6:17, it told us to take the helmet of salvation and the sword of the Spirit. I believe it is the combination of the two that must work together. We must be identified through our salvation in Christ. If not, then who are we? That's the enemy's response when we prematurely wield the sword of God without having a personal relationship with Christ. I've said many times before, we cannot operate in spiritual matters without the Spirit. Through salvation, we received the Spirit. With this Spirit, like King Arthur pulling the sword out of the rock, we may rightly wield the Word of God and attack our enemies.

So through receiving salvation, which is received through profession and believing that Jesus Christ is Lord and Savior, we likewise wield the sword of the Spirit by continuing to profess and believe in the Word of God. Read and meditate over God's word. Give charge to the angels to honor God's Word, to demolish the enemy for God's namesake. As for me and my house, we will serve the Lord! Many of the afflictions of the righteous, but God delivers them from them all! No weapon formed against me shall prosper! Nay, in all things, we are more than conquerors!

My mind was literally attacked the night I wrote this chapter, spiraling down this continuous vision of barrenness, strife, and violence in my home. I finally jumped out of my dream and declared 2 Corinthians 10:5:

We demolish arguments and every pretension that sets itself up against the knowledge of God, we take captive every thought to make it obedient to Christ.

I said it a couple of times, afterwards, my mind was at peace and I went back to sleep. Wielding the Word of God works!

Another way that love protects is that it defends. Whereas in attacking, the energy is directed at the enemy, in defending, the energy is directed at the one being protected.

Who will bring any charge against those who God has chosen? It is God who justifies. Who then is the one who condemns? No one. Christ Jesus who died - more than that, who was raised to life - is at the right hand of God and is also interceding for us.

Intercede means to act or to interpose in behalf of someone in difficulty or trouble, as by pleading or petition. In our relationships, there will be times when our mates veer off course. They may be faced with great struggles; they may have made some mistakes, but who is to condemn them if we have chosen them? Love always protects. We should go before God and thank Him for His grace, and we should ask for His mercy to shine down on our mates. God, my wife is still the one you love. God, her husband is still the man you love. Have mercy on them. Withhold your judgment and redeem him/her from the trial. Let your glory and love shine down on us. Remain faithful, especially now. I'm standing in the gap, by the power of your spirit, remaining faithful. Honor the efforts of this your servant. Allow us to triumph over this time in this season. Do not allow Satan or the world to mock at us. Reveal your face and deliver your humble son and daughter. By Christ Jesus present us pure and righteous.

Are you interceding? Revelations 12:10 refers to Satan as "the accuser of our brothers and sisters, who accuses them before God day and night." Do not join forces with Satan and accuse your spouse. Do not join the world and label them based on their mistakes. Defend them!
In the Bible, Saul had persecuted many Christians, even caused some to be put to death. Yet, God called him into his service. Ananias recalled all that Saul had done, but in Acts 9:15, God commands and states:

This man is my chosen instrument to proclaim my name to the Gentiles and their kings and to the people of Israel.

Our mates will have some Saul moments in their lives. We will have some Saul moments in our lives: misguided actions inflicting harm on each other. But through revelation and wisdom, God places those misguided actions on the right side and invites us to serve a righteous purpose in the process.

The next way love protects is more of a proactive approach to defending - covering. I Peter 4:7 – 8 states:

Above all, love each other deeply, because love covers a multitude of sins [overlooks unkindness and unselfishly seeks the best for others].

In Luke 22:31 – 32, Jesus says:

Simon, Simon, listen! Satan has demanded permission to sift [all of you] like grain; but I have prayed [especially] for you [Peter], that your faith [and confidence in Me] may not fail; and you, when you have turned back again [to Me], strengthen and support your brothers [in the faith].

In the Scripture, Jesus is aware that Peter would deny Him and abandon Him in the most distressed time of His mortal life. Peter hasn't even done it yet, but Jesus has already prayed for him, sought to have him return to Him, and has given him a call upon his return.

The reality, even in our relationships, is that we will turn away from each other from time to time, sometimes for a short moment, and even possibly for a season. Are we proactively praying for reunion, strength and courage for these times and seasons? Are we proactively praying for the well-being of our mates, even if they would be the ones who turn away? Are we praying that we will deeply love them to the point we can overlook the unkindness and desire the best outcomes for them?

Without this covering, we are left vulnerable to attacks. Satan will demand permission to sift out our flaws and imperfections. It will happen on both personal and relational platforms. Without the covering, all that we will experience is shame. You will feel disconnected, damaged, and no longer qualified to dwell in the union. Yet, a covering appoints a time and place to establish a reunion. In John, chapter 21, Jesus has an opportunity to be before Peter after Jesus had fulfilled his purpose. Jesus asked Peter three times if Peter loved him, "with a deep personal affection, as for a close friend," in which Peter responded that he did. Peter surely reflected on his denying Jesus, but Jesus allowed him to reaffirm his love for him, to be at peace with the past, and to move forward in purpose.

If we fail to do this in our relationships, when we fall (which we will) we will not only fall but fail. Love always protects, and in that protection, love covers. If we were eating a meal or making lunch plans, if you suggested a place I couldn't afford, with generosity, you may tell me, "Don't worry about it. I've got you covered." In essence you are saying "I know you can't pay for it, so I will incur the debt." Are we preparing to incur each other's debt - mistakes we really can't afford to pay for? Gaps in our wisdom and understanding? Reactions to our hurt, pain and past? Are we covering each other, so though the enemy has been granted permission to strike, we already have a healing process set up?

WHAT IS LOVE

When countries go to war, they send medics with the soldiers. They understand that there is a high and likely possibility for injuries. The closer the medic is to the scene, the more likely is the chance for survival. Keep healing close to your relationships. Through trials and tribulations, it is likely that you will need it.

Lastly, another way love protects is to flee from danger. Proverbs 27:12 states:

The prudent see danger and take refuge, but the simple keep going and pay the penalty.

In relationships, in the presence of the three major enemies, some battles are won by simply avoiding them. For instance, there are things we know we struggle with, in our flesh, yet we will walk towards areas where we know we would have to fight. We over indulge in alcohol, yet we socialize in areas where alcohol is popularly served. We lust, yet we follow media sources that employ the ideas of sex or sexual images. We indulge in gossip which also draws negativity, yet we watch shows infused with gossip and drama. So many battles that could easily be won by simply distancing ourselves away from them. I Corinthians 6:18 states:

Flee from sexual immorality. All other sins a person commits are outside the body, but whoever sins sexually, sins against their own body.

Now in Ecclesiasticus... that is right - Ecclesiasticus, not Ecclesiastes, 21:2 - It says:

Flee from Satan as from the face of a serpent: for if thou comest too near it, it will bite thee.

This scripture is in the King James Version with the Apocrypha. I think it is wise to take heed to the verse. Sin will snap at you with the reflexes of a snake and with equal venom. To protect our relationships and ourselves, we should stay away from the sinful areas as much as possible. In this way, we protect the health and well-being of our spirits in our relationships. Remember, the serpent was there to persuade the first sin through temptation.

If we pay attention to our spirits close enough, we will sense it tell us to back down, go the other way, hold our tongue, and flee. We must become disciplined in adhering to that voice. In doing so, we weaken the enemy. We refrain from slipping into his snare.

Love always protects, attacking the enemy with the word of God, defending our loved ones through intercession, covering through anticipated trials and falls, fleeing from discovered traps and dangers. Without protection, we are left vulnerable to the attacks of the enemy, who doesn't want God to have any glory and therefore doesn't want you and especially marriage to succeed. The enemy understands the residual effects of taking down just one home, just one heart.

Proverbs 4:23 instructs us in saying *guard your hearts, for everything you do flows from it.* If the enemy successfully infiltrates our hearts, what will we subject ourselves to doing?

Proverbs 23:7 says *for as a man thinks in his heart, so is he.* If we allow the world to convince us that love doesn't matter and that marriage is a prison, we further shadow the image God desired to create through man. Let's protect God's image of man, God's image and example of love, and God's purpose for marriage. Let's walk in the spirit of love and the one who gave his life to call us brothers and sisters, to extend an invitation to God's holy kingdom and inherit his righteousness and his glory. Let's wield His word, walk in His compassion, and meet each trial in our relationships with triumph.

Us vs. Them

They don't want us to succeed.
They don't want us to believe.
They want us to succumb to their greed.
They sell false promises to enable selfishness to bereave.
They attack everything we celebrate. Where we choose love they choose hate.
Everything that love builds they attempt to eradicate.
Inundated with all of the trials that life deals, they work to intimidate.
They don't want us to live in true peace.
They don't want the fighting and feuding to cease.
They don't want to see us build a legacy.
They attack us with fervent hatred fueled by their jealousy.
But we will continue to fight to protect our hearts.
We will continue to use faith to shield us from their fiery darts.
We will use God's word to cut through their lies and accusations.
We will flee from perceived dangers to arrive safely at our destinations.
We will continue to cover each other and have each other's backs.

We will lean on each other's strengths to be stronger together than apart, defending us from all of their attacks.
We are set up for victory as long as we remember that God is on our side.
In the safety of His arms our hearts must abide.

CHAPTER 12:
Love Always Trusts

My children are fascinating. Both of them could be considered to be daredevils or perhaps very physically active. They love to swing, climb, jump and wrestle. It doesn't help that they considered me to be more of a jungle gym than that of my wife. I've had many impromptu workout sessions, and so has my wife. The crazy thing about it is that they are, in fact, even more adventurous when I'm around than when I'm not. My daughter likes for me to throw her onto the bed - the stronger I launch her, the more she enjoys it. She likes to be spun around and, even when she was younger, she'd love to run to the edge of the bed and dive off so that I would catch her in my arms. As she has gotten older, she now likes to make that gap before the jump wider and wider. My son likes to climb on me as if he's hiking up my extremities, using the force behind his legs to push away with every step. I literally have to use every bit of force to keep him from launching his body

Love Always Trusts

like a projectile off my chest. He then tilts the upper part of his body back as I hold onto his shoulders and arms. Then, he proceeds to conduct a back flip back onto the surface of the ground. He, like my daughter, likes to be spun around and tossed into the air. What amazes me the most is how he'll walk off the edge of couches and beds without prompting, just because I'm near.

Again, it is fascinating and perhaps horrifying all at the same time. Doesn't he know he could fall? What if I don't notice that he's taking a dive? What if I can't get there in time? What if I accidentally drop him? Yet, time after time, he does all of this without hesitation and I began to realize just how much he trusts me to be there for him, to catch him before he falls, and to guide him through his motions. Beyond the questions that I may have, he has chosen to live by this statement: "I trust my father."

Love always trusts. There are so many unknowns and uncertainties in love and dating. Is it really safe to proverbially jump off the edge of the bed? Will we be caught or will we fall? The danger beyond falling is that, while it is wise to be cautious and have boundaries in dating, there comes a time when one must make a jump into the unknown, uncertain of the outcome. If you allow them, uncertainties, doubts and fears can have you paralyzed or better yet cleaving to the ground beneath you, shrieking if anybody even attempts to move you from where you are - your comfort zone.

Some of us feel we have every right and reason to be cautious. We believe it is foolish to be so trusting. We've trusted before. We took the jump and fell flat on our faces. We were cheated, manipulated, mistreated, abused, disrespected, unloved, abandoned, rejected, and forgotten about. You couldn't pay some of us enough money to believe in love again. "Love cannot guarantee I will not get hurt again." "Love didn't keep them here." "Love left me with heartbreak." "Love has left me by myself."

    Then there are those of us who can't even trust ourselves. We have never been faithful in a relationship. We run at the sight of commitment. We were too selfish and independent to make the needed sacrifices. Our self-esteem is too low to be who we need to be in a relationship. Our wallets are too empty. Our dreams are too undefined or distant. Our pasts are too heavy. I present is too troubled. What can we trust ourselves to do but cause problems and disappoint? We're so sure that we are going to let them down and mistreat them. To some of us, not even love can handle what we have going on. We strived to do things the right way before and have failed, miserably. There are no promises that it won't happen again. In fact, we feel like it is almost likely that we will fail again. How are we going to just jump off the edge and expect not to fall? Yet, I Corinthians 13 tells us that love always trust: not sometimes or occasionally. How is that even possible?

    Trust is the reliance on the integrity, strength, ability and surety of a person or a thing. It is the hope placed in someone or something. We rely on the people and things we place our trust. Though love always trusts, we live in a time where people find it hard to trust love. It is difficult to trust each other. It is really difficult to believe in the certainty of anything. We really just don't know what may happen. We have no confidence in anything. Once we are let down, each time we are let down, we lose a bit more confidence in love, in people and in ourselves. How is it that love manages to always trusts?

Trust in the Lord with all your heart and lean not unto your own understanding; in all your ways submit to him, and he will make your paths straight. ~ Proverbs 3:5

This scripture does well at defining the posture of true trust. It enforces trusting with all of your heart, not part of it. Indeed, I believe it is a process to operating in absolute trust. One of the main setbacks is relying on your own understanding, because in every pocket of misunderstanding, if will lean in on our own, we will not submit our ways to that of what we're trusting in or who we are trusting in. This definitely comes in play in areas where we need to be selfless, kind, humble, generous and forgiving. If we don't understand or buy into the why, we fail to submit our ways to the call even in our relationships where we profess to love the one we are with.

Another thing this scripture reveals is that the more we allow ourselves to trust, the quicker we can arrive at our desired destinations. He said that it will make our paths straight. The shortest distance between any two points is a straight line. Many things we desire in our relationships could be achieved and obtained through less turmoil and time if we operate in trust. Without trust, we waver in our paths.

And lastly, yet most importantly, the scripture reveals who to put our trust into: the Lord. Many times, if we reflect back on where life has stained our image of love and relationships, we discovered that it was not God who failed us. It wasn't even love, either. We put our trust in ourselves, thinking we could handle everything on our own. We trusted our emotions and our feelings. We trusted that the activities we engaged in were bringing us closer: the premarital sex or even innocent things like hanging out and enjoying conversations. We thought those things were good enough and directing enough. Normally, the bumps on the roads proved devastating when we didn't respond the way we felt the Spirit prompting us to, so we veered off the path. We were supposed to forgive but we didn't. We were supposed to refrain from sex but we didn't. We were supposed to get counseling but we didn't. To our understandings, these things weren't dire or important enough to follow.

Love understands this truth. God desires our absolute trust because he set the path to those things He's promised us, and no one knows better than Him how to obtain them. He will allow us to watch everything else we've entrusted to fall short of His promises before relinquishing His glory to false hope.

When you cry out for help, let your collection of idols save you! The wind will carry all of them off, a mere breath will blow them away. But whoever takes refuge in me will inherit the land and possess my holy mountain.
~Isaiah 57:13

God is not denying the blessings in our love lives. He designed marriage. He covenanted relationships. He wants us to have them. However, we cannot reap the blessings by trusting the world's way of receiving them. We even fall short by putting our absolute trust in each other. Face it, we are human and we will let each other down from time to time, even in huge ways. If we aren't walking with our trust in the Lord in those seasons, we will bail out because we don't understand how those things were able to happen, and one could only dare to suggest that we keep on moving forward together.

The Scripture reveals, that when our trust is misplaced, it doesn't even take much for those things to be revealed as incompetent: our looks, our intelligence, our money, and our connections. All of these things ultimately will crumble at the mere winds of life. When it happens, we get frustrated at love because our relationships have failed, but love never told us to put our trust in those things.

Such confidence we have through Christ before God, not that we are competent in ourselves to claim anything for ourselves, but our competence comes from God. He has made us competent as ministers of a new covenant - not of the letter but that of the Spirit; for the letter kills, but the Spirit gives life. ~2 Corinthians 3:46

We are not to be competent in ourselves but we are to place competence in our spirits which are guided, instructed and directed by God.

Command those who are rich in this present world not to be arrogant nor to put their hope in wealth, which is so uncertain, but to put their hope in God, who richly provides everything for our enjoyment. ~ I Timothy 6:17

This scripture is richly important. So many individuals offset companionship these days and cleave to wealth (or the pursuit of it) as a substitute. So many couples spend the bulk of their energy on jobs as opposed to working on their relationship with God and each other, and as a result they never find enjoyment. Wealth is so uncertain; however, even without wealth, God richly provides us with not just some but everything for our enjoyment, but we have to trust him to do so.

We tend to put too much pressure on each other and our relationships to provide our enjoyment. We basically set each other up for failure. Sure enough, God can and will provide some of this enjoyment through our relationship but we should always check our source of this enjoyment.

We have discussed how the blessings flow from always trusting in God, and now we will discuss the meat of why I believe love always trusts.

The fear of man will prove to be a snare, but whoever trusts in the Lord is kept safe.
~Proverbs 29:25

Love realizes it cannot operate in fear. Ultimately, it would find itself trapped and unable to function. As we all know, there is a fear of intimacy in this world, to be vulnerable and proverbially naked before someone; faults, flaws and all. We fear the opinion of man and rejection. We take upon coldness as a defense mechanism, closing ourselves off from living in our aspirations just to merely survive.

God can save our relationships from whatever we may face.

Surely God is my salvation;
I will trust and not be afraid. The Lord, the Lord himself, is my strength and defense; he has become my salvation.
~ Isaiah 12:2

See, we fear in relationships or operate in fear when we stop trusting God. It is not a lack of trust in ourselves or our mates that is the ultimate problem. It is our lack of trust in God. Trusting in God supplies us with strength in times of battle. "The communication is off in my relationship but I trust God. I have strength for the battle." "Intimacy is foreign in my marriage, but I trust God to richly provide all enjoyment. I have strength for the battle." "We lost a house." "We lost the baby." "We are barely paying bills, but I put my trust in God. I have strength for the battle."

The Scripture says that the Lord himself is my defense, my protection. It may appear that I'm not enough but God defends my identity. Seems like my faults are great, but God defends me. My family, my relationship, and my character are being attacked, but I trust God and he will defend me.

I will save you; you will not fall by the sword, but will escape with your life, because you trust in me, declares the Lord. ~ Jeremiah 39:18

Every relationship goes to something that tries to take them out: a spouse is unfaithful, discord is in the home, hurt has reached a peak, or complacency has set in. New challenges and new dangers are on every side. We know this world doesn't want love to thrive. We know Satan doesn't want relationships to survive, but if we put our trust in God, we will escape with our lives. We will not fall by the sword. God can save our relationships from whatever we may face, if we trust Him to and if we submit our whole selves into His process. Victory is at the end of the path. We will overcome trial after trial, test after test, attack after attack, and all the adversity if we trust.

WHAT IS LOVE

Those who trust in the Lord are like Mount Zion, which cannot be shaken but endures forever. ~ Psalms 125:1

Love will not be shaken. If we operate in love we would not be shaken. "Yes, it hurt sometimes, but my commitment is not shaken. I'm here. I'm in love with you. I don't know what tomorrow holds. I don't want to lose you, but today you're here, my presence is not shaken. I am here to love you."

Here's the thing. God will allow life to test your trust in Him. He, in effect, wants to reveal to us who we are what we are really made of through the trying of our faith.

Indeed, we felt we had received a sentence of death. This happened that we might not rely on ourselves but on God, who raises the dead. He has delivered us from such a deadly peril, and he will deliver us again.
~ 2 Corinthians 9:10

In relationships and marriages, we will face death. Everything will seem like the end, like it is all over, like there is nothing else in our might we can do, and that is okay. In fact, it is perfectly fine. It isn't a situation that we are qualified to handle. It doesn't mean that it won't work out; it means it is a set up by design for God to be the only one qualified to work it out. If we trust in God, we don't have to worry about how dead our marriages are or how dead our relationships are, because God raises the dead! Nothing is more life-giving than to be dead then alive again, to come from the lowest point and breathe again, smile again, laugh again, and have dreams again. God can deliver relationships and he will not only do it once, but he will deliver us again!

Love always trusts. Love knows that God is reliable. His strength is undeniable. His promises are made good. Love cannot confidently operate without trusting God. Love operates without fear because of its trust in God, and we, in our relationships, wherever we presently are, can do the same.

I Trust You

Lord, there is no problem too big for you.
I trust You to help us overcome everything that we will go through.
Even when I doubt myself I know that you order our steps; I'm never too proud to ask for help.
I won't be persuaded by feelings that are felt. I let go of any inner vows that have been kept.
I trust you to deliver us even in the darkest of times.
Keep your word in my mind so that my faith in you remains sublime.
You are faithful in all seasons. Pain will never be a strong enough reason to give up on what you trying to accomplish in my life.
You are a present help. I trust you to give me the strength, wisdom and love to be there for my wife.

CHAPTER 13:
Love Always Hopes

Hope - to look forward to with desire and reasonable confidence, to believe, desire or trust.

    You know, I believe we misconstrue hope with wishing and maybe even worrying. Better yet, I believe we do more focusing on hope as a noun but rarely execute it in its verb form, and, even then, the measure of it is faint. We hope we get a promotion or raise on a job, yet in the interim of time, we stress and worry how bills would be paid. We hope loved ones will get better in health yet we dread phone calls anticipating that one that will be to state that they have passed on.

    We hope one day we'll find the right one, yet we pursue relationships with so much hesitation and reluctance. We hope we are good enough but we walk with a lack of confidence and in low self-esteem. We hope the relationship will work out, yet we walk on eggshells as if it is going to fall apart at any moment. Is that really what hope looks like? Or we really believing? Are you really looking forward to those things or are we really expecting to be let down, disappointed and denied? Do we ever use hope in a statement and speak with confidence? The truth is, most of the time, it is out of concern or worry. "I hope one day I'll find love because right now, I don't really know." "I hope the relationship will work out, but I honestly feel like it is not." "I hope one day, I'll be happy because I can't remember the last time I was."

The problem isn't in acknowledging that those things haven't come to pass. In fact, things that haven't happened yet or the only things we can hope for.

> Be courageous in the face of trials.

For in this hope we were saved. But hope that is seen is no hope at all. Who hopes for what they already have? But if we hope for what we do not have, we wait for it patiently. ~ Romans 8:24-25

It is okay to acknowledge what hasn't happened yet. The problem is genuine hope has the character of confidence and belief and rarely do we use the word hope in confidence and as an expression of belief. We hope things will happen, but we are not going to hold our breath while waiting. Worry and hope do not mix. Fear and hope do not mix. Yet, anxious prayers or used daily, masked as hope. For that reason, we are not compelled to hope, for where at the root anxiety thrives, hope is admonished.

Love always hopes, genuinely - not this worry, not this anxiety, and not this feeble wishing and praying. Love confidently believes that things that have not happened yet will come to pass. "I have hope that one day, I will overcome my hurts." "I have hope that one day, I'll understand how God intended for us to love." "I have hope that one day I'll marry the person of my dreams." "I have hope that one day, our marriage will overcome this bad place we are in." "I have hope that we will celebrate fifty years of bliss." Here's the thing. If it is not igniting a fire of desire, then it is not hope. If you're walking around feeling defeated and downtrodden, you are not operating out of a place of hope.

Why, my soul, or you downcast? Why so disturbed within me? Put your hope in God, for I will yet praise him, my Savior and my God. ~ Psalms 42:5

In life, including in our relationships, it is natural, if not promised to face some things that attempt to pull our souls down. Finances, intimacy, communication, hurts, losses, and confusion will all be right in our faces. When we feel ourselves getting pulled down, we need to talk to ourselves just as in the example in the scripture and ask why are we so down. Where is our hope?

If we can only feel good about life in our relationships when things are good in the present, we will not go the distance. We will fold. Satan already doesn't want you to get married and have a flourishing relationship. He's going to throw everything at you and watch all your joy, all of your happiness, and all of your passion just flee from you.

Be strong and take heart, all you who hope in the Lord. ~Psalms 31:24

Be courageous in the face of trials. Be courageous in the face of hurts and in the face of doubts. Put your hope in God and be strong. Love understands tribulations are inevitable. Keep living. There will come a time in your relationship when all odds will be stacked up against it. There will come a time in your relationship when it feels like the gates of hell or prevailing against it. "We aren't speaking anymore." He hasn't even looked your way in months. She hasn't even touched you in months. It's been a year since you've been on a date. "We are walking around our home like mere roommates, strangers even."

"Everything in front of us is trying to tell is that it is not going to work out." Right in that moment, it is the perfect time to close your eyes because hope isn't looking at what is in front of it. Hope looks at whom hope has been placed, believing desires and needs are being met. Love knows with hope, it can close its eyes and keep walking and keep moving forward, because it understands that by doing so it gets the attention of Almighty God.

But the eyes of the Lord are on those whose hope is in his unfailing love, to deliver them from death and keep them alive in famine. ~Psalms 33:18

If your relationship is in a famine season then say these words: "So I may not be receiving a lot of love from my mate, but God, your unfailing love is more than sufficient. I will live through this famine season. We will not die. We will live." When we keep our hope in God, we find ourselves nourished even in famine. We will live. In hope, the testing and trials do not weigh down our health as it attempts. Our hearts do not harden. Our spirits continue to thrive despite the calamity and displeasure. When we stand on God's words, we find comfort.

Remember your word to your servant, for you have given me hope. My comfort in my suffering is this: Your promise preserves my life.
~Psalms 119:45-50

Love knows that the sufferings don't have to eat away at our lives. If we hold on to God's promises, we can maintain expectant desire. Many people who have gotten a tattoo have experienced a discomfort, if not actual pain, but they endure it in anticipation of the final product. They hope it turns out just as they desired. They also know, if they tap out, the product will be incomplete.

Don't let mere discomforts and pain cause you to tap out. Love will never be able to model a complete work if we continue to do that. God has a promise to those who are faithful, to those that continue to trust in Him. Don't get me wrong. It can be challenging to trust God in trying times, especially when we've wronged each other. Let's be honest, in those seasons we tend to put our lack of hope in each other above our hope in God. Sin and the frailty of man tend to work its way in between us and those things we were confidently pursuing. "Maybe this isn't meant to be." "Are we supposed to be having these kind of problems?" "Maybe something is wrong with us."

When the offenses are severe, it is difficult at times to regain hope. Yes, it may be difficult, but not impossible. In fact, there is hope for both the offender and the offended. God can restore both to a place of renewed hope and desire.

And I have the same hope in God as these men themselves have, that there will be a resurrection, both the righteous and the wicked. ~Acts 24:15

Jesus had come to give them both eternal life, resurrecting them from the dead. Likewise, God is more than capable and desiring to redeem both the offender and the offended.

Yet if you devote your heart to him and stretch out your hands to him, if you put away the sin that is in your hand and allow no evil to dwell in your tent, then, free of fault, you will lift up your face; you will stand firm and without fear. You will surely forget your trouble recalling it only as waters gone by. Life will be brighter than noonday, and darkness will become like morning. You'll be secure because there is hope; you will look about you and take your rest and safety. You will lie down, with no one to make you afraid, and many will court your favor. But the eyes of the wicked will fail, and escape will elude them; their hope will become a dying gasp. ~Job 11:13

Indeed, there is hope for the transgressor. In here, God has provided a roadmap and a promise to those who have done wrong in the relationship. Before we recall what that roadmap is, I want to first emphasize that God points out that not following his plan leads to demise. We can't continue in sin and witness the fruition of hope. Our own actions become a contradiction to what we profess to desire. God directs us to give Him our hearts and stretch out our hands to Him. He wants us to fully surrender ourselves: everything that drives us in our actions and thoughts. Allow Him to guide us. He says to allow no evil to dwell in our tents. Though we are only at this place for a season, before we pick up our tent and move forward, we must remove the evil things that motivated the sin: jealousy, pride, lust, and idolatry. Those things will continue to attempt to enslave us and lead us to walk in defeat, all in which no hope can be established.

God says that the offender can be free of fault. God has shown us that we can overcome the sin, and that we are not our sin. With our hearts in His hand, we are stronger than the evil that drove us to sin. We don't have to be afraid of sinning again. We only see it as a battle won. We now have hope. We can safely believe in ourselves again. The Bible says that many will seek out our favor. People familiar with our troubles get to witness the new us and how we walk, now, closer with God. People will now want that for themselves.

If you have done wrong in your relationship, there is still hope for you. Give your heart over to God. Walk away from the sin. Trust God to introduce your significant other to a new you, but let God create that transformation first.

It is not guilt that will redeem your relationship, but it is the hope, being redeemed by God and acknowledging that you don't have to live in your troubles but in the new spirit God creates in your heart. God can cause the stubborn hurt to fall off your significant other's heart. With a life brighter than the noonday, and darkness like the morning, they would not be able to do anything but see you. You'll be able to live without fear, secure in the new place God has brought you to.

For the one that has suffered in the relationship, there is hope for you, too.

We also glory in our suffering, because we know that suffering produces perseverance; perseverance character, and character hope. ~Romans 5:3-4

As stated before, if problems drive us to bail out, our character is the greater problem. Every relationship faces extreme circumstances. We have to come to a place where we are genuinely committed to press on through the difficult seasons. In these problematic circumstances, there are unique jewels of opportunity. In this season, we show genuine, authentic compassion, selflessness, forgiveness and strength. We have the opportunity to hang in there like Christ did for us. "It hurts. I possibly didn't deserve it. You don't even know the weight of what you're doing right now, but I have a purpose to fulfill, to love you, anyway, to cover your sin for a greater glory. When we have overcome this, as I have remained faithfully committed and have been able to reap the fruit of victory over this season. I'll see all the more what I'm made of. I'll see all the more what we are capable of overcoming. I can have hope. I don't have to worry about problems for I can always see victory and reconciliation on the other side. I am stronger than the sufferings. I can live without fear. I am not the victim. I can own my choice to stay, my strength to endure, and my courage to press forward. I've experienced spiritual maturity and can walk in spiritual authority. I can now see that I am fit for the battle. I am not worried about the tears because I can see us smiling again. I see us coming out of this being even closer, more vulnerable, and more convinced." We should all desire to hope and have the strength to make this decree!

Pride and fear like to creep up into the spirits of the offended. No one wants to play the fool. But Romans 5:5 encourages us in this:

Hope does not put us to shame, because God's love has been poured out into our hearts through the Holy Spirit, who has been given to us.

It is okay to believe that God will answer your prayers and your desires to see your relationship work out. The Holy Spirit can guide you to that place of reconciliation. And yes, once again, it can be hard, but stop complaining. Yes, it can be difficult, but stop fearing. Be strong. Be courageous. Be convinced!

As for me, I will always have hope. I will praise you more and more. ~Psalms 71:14

Remember Psalms 42:5 said I "put my hope in God, for I will yet praise him..." If you are struggling to find hope or tap into your hope, the Word of God is insisting on you making the time and effort to praise Him. To offer praise is to demonstrate gratitude. It sets our minds on what God has already done which can then usher us into what we believe He's doing and will do. Basically, our praise will fuel our hope, and if we aren't praising, it may very well be killing all hope.

A lot of times, we stop showing gratitude towards God and each other in our relationships. We focus on problems or on what we don't have and we have failed to acknowledge what we do have. I believe that if we praise God for what we do have, we can have hope for those things we don't have yet. Some of you reading this might be saying "You just don't know how bad it is. We're basically on our way out. All of the signs point to an exit. All of the energy says that this is the end. The love is gone. The relationship is dead. The situation is helpless."

Against all hope, Abraham in hope believed and so became the father of many nations, just as it had been said to him, "so shall your offspring be" without weakening in his faith, he faced the fact that his body was as good as dead (since he was about 100 years old) and that Sarah's womb was also dead. Yet he did not waver through unbelief regarding the promise of God, but was strengthened in faith and gave glory to God, being fully persuaded that God had power to do what he had promised. ~Romans 4:18

I love that we can acknowledge the facts about our situations and we can still have hope. Against all hope, Abraham chose to still hope. We know ultimately that which he trusted God for came to pass, against all of the natural odds. Likewise, no matter how dead the situations make our relationships appear to be, we can choose to have hope, that God can help us overcome. Hope will give us strength for the battle and the journey. We can fight for our relationships. Acknowledge the challenges but do not focus on them. Place greater value on what God can accomplish through us.

Do not count yourself out from having hope. Ecclesiastes 9:4 reads "anyone who is among the living has hope - even the live dog is better than a dead lion!" There is hope for us all, and there is no glory or purpose without fully allowing God to utilize us as examples of His strength, His love and His glory. Love always hopes. It is not about what we are capable of, but what God is capable of. He's aware of our shortcomings. He's not asking us to do it in our own might. He equips us for the journey.

May the God of hope fill you with all joy and peace as you trust in him, so that you may overflow with hope by the power of the Holy Spirit.
~ Romans 15:13

This hope is a powerful source; let love walk in it. Let's not pursue life in worry and uncertainty. Walk through it with confident expectancy. There is hope for us in all of the seasons of our relationships. Trust God's words and His commandments. There is joy and peace there. We don't have to be afraid. God will not be put to shame. We may see the facts, but hope sees that in all things we are more than conquerors. In hope, our problems won't conquer us, we'll overcome them!

Hope Supplies

*There are so many great things coming our way; I can see them with my eyes closed.
We may not currently possess all the necessary things to get there, but we're still in a good position because God knows.
I don't need to lean on my doubt because I doubt God could ever fail at His word.
Even when things seem impossible, to think God would not deliver sounds more absurd.
When life and circumstances build walls around our dreams, we'll march around them and let out a big shout.
When Goliaths of trouble stand in our way, we will show up for the battle believing God is already given us the bout.
In the presence of so many enemies and uncertainties, hope supplies us with the energy to see it through.
We will continue to be triumphant and victorious. Our God is so glorious and His word remains true.*

CHAPTER 14:
Love Always Perseveres

    In conversation, I've told this story so many times before, but it never gets old to me. It has made an everlasting impression on me. Though experienced in my childhood, the lesson learned is as relevant if not even more relevant to me as an adult. It was my eighth grade year in junior high. I was finally climbing out of my shell, adjusting to what was considered cool at the time. In the presence of such fulfillment, school began to evolve from its simple function of academics and good grades to a more social and extracurricular experience. My crushes reached new heights. My interactions with fellow students became more sociable and free. Desires and passions began to emerge from the mundane expectations, one in which was football.

    I love football. It is such an exciting sport to watch and play. I played often in the neighborhood, but I had never wore kneepads, shoulder pads and a helmet. I never ran the span of a football field, ran towards end zones as crowds cheered, or intercepted a football shifting the direction of the other twenty-one players on the field. Genetically, I've always been on the slimmer side. All of the players I saw on TV looked so big. Nonetheless, my eighth grade year, I made a decision. I wanted to try out for the football team. I informed my parents and they agreed to allow it.

Coach Walton. I will never forget his name. Everyone knew he was a no nonsense, tough coach. On the initial tryout day, we stood in a line with our shirts off, waiting to be seen by the coach, perhaps for placing us in specific categories or positions, or to be fitted for our practice equipment. As I walked up to Coach Walton, he exclaimed to another coach, "We have another birdie on our hands!" Of course, I didn't bring a bird to tryouts; he was speaking of my small chest size. That moment was very motivating for me, just kidding.

Fast-forward time, my parents found an inexpensive pair of cleats, the school provided the practice gear and I was assigned a locker. I was officially trying out for the team. I remember running around the football field till I literally puked. I remember being so small and long that my practice gear would hang off of me. I remember being clumsy, falling over other teammates, as the sprinklers weighed down my already big pants. I remember trying to get out of the car after practice and I'd catch cramps, at the same time, in both of my calve muscles. I remember waking up in the middle of the night to those same cramps as I clasped my pillow until they went away. I stayed in my room. I felt alone. I felt like a failure. I wished my dad was more involved, more vocal, and more encouraging.

One day, Coach Walton informs us of a mandatory practice. If anybody missed this practice, they would automatically be off of the team. It just so happened that I had a dentist appointment on that same day. I wouldn't be coming to school at all on that day. I didn't tell the coach about my dentist appointment, and I didn't my parents about the mandatory practice. When I returned to school the following day and went to practice, my locker was cleaned out. Till this day, I don't even know where they put my cleats. I spoke with Coach Walton and explained that I missed practice because of the dentist appointment. With no emotion, he simply said that I should've told him beforehand. It was permanent. I was off the team.

A few weeks after that, tryouts were over. The team was set. One of the people that tried out was in my class. He was shorter than me an equally slim. Somehow, however, he made the team. To my recollection, he hadn't stood out in practice. I was completely astonished. I had to know how he made the team, so I asked him what did he do to make the team. His answer was simple. "I just didn't quit," he said.

Here's the thing. Coach Walton's mandatory practice was just a set up to give those, who wanted to quit, an easy way out. At the end of the day, it wasn't the puking, it wasn't the cramping, it wasn't the too big practice uniform, it wasn't my dad's lack of words, and it wasn't Coach Walton being out to get me. It was me, my choices, that kept me from my dreams, my passions, and my love. I gave up. I quit. I counted myself out from something I could have very well had. I decided not to endure, not to persevere.

Love always endures. So many times relationships fail because the trials and tribulations outweigh our commitments. We give up on our desires. We tend to focus on everything we don't have and everything that is not working well for us. We give those things priority over desire, over passion, and over love.

We blame our circumstances, we blame our pasts, we blame the other person, but at the end of the day, it is our choice to quit and to give up which keeps us from what would otherwise be promised to us. This is where we and love go separate ways. We stopped walking together. We quit while love still desires to fight and to press forward.

We lean on how discouraged our flesh is in being unfulfilled and ignore our spirits desire to love anyhow and to give anyhow. Our minds are convinced it is over; love says we are just beginning. We haven't seen our best days yet. We can make the team if we just don't quit. Despite whatever we may face in the pursuit of love and relationships, love always perseveres.

Persevere - to persist in anything undertaken; maintain a purpose in spite of difficulty, obstacles or discouragement; continue steadfastly.

You know, when I tried out for the team, the purpose was to fulfill the heartfelt desire I had. The pain, the difficulties, and the obstacles took my focus off the purpose. I focused on the pain. I kept it at the forefront of my mind. I developed fear, doubt and discouragement. It wasn't that I didn't love football anymore. It was that I wanted the pain to go away.

So many times we bail out of relationships because we just want the pain to go away. We want to rid ourselves of the fear, doubt and discouragement. We're tired of arguing. We are tired of fighting. We're tired of feeling unloved. We are tired of the lack of communication. We're tired of the lack of intimacy. We're tired of dealing with their faults. We are tired of feeling like a failure in relationships, and we just want the pain to go away.

WHAT IS LOVE

Consider it pure joy, my brothers and sisters, whenever you face trials of many kinds, because you know that the testing of your faith produces perseverance. Let perseverance finish its work so that you may be mature and complete, not lacking anything. ~James 1:2-4

    If I had just stayed on the team, those aching calve muscles would've been strong. I would've had the cardio to run up and down the field to catch and intercept passes. I would've had the wisdom of organized football: the play calling, the positions, and the reads. I'd learn how to get up after getting knocked down. I would've learned how to sacrifice myself, to face pain to gain an extra yard, and to press forward towards first downs and end zones. I would have conquered and overcome the pain - the pain that convinced me that I was unworthy of what I deeply desired.

    In the same likeness, if we just persevere in our relationships, we would develop that patience by overcoming time. We would gain that selflessness that draws us closer together. We'd developed the respect to address each other appropriately. We would discover 1001 ways to be intimate in any season. We'd face the pain of getting knocked down, build the strength to get back up, and sacrifice self just to move a little closer in love. We'd face all the pain that attempted to divide us and overcome it with faith and with conviction, calling it the lie that it is. "Pain, you got it wrong. If you think you can separate me from the love of my life, you are mistaken! In this I have purpose now and I will not forfeit purpose to alleviate pain." If we deferred purpose, we would live out an eternal pain.

Do not be afraid of what you are about to suffer. I tell you, the devil will put some of you in prison to test you, and you will suffer persecution for ten days. Be faithful, even to the point of death, and I will give you life as your victor's crown. ~Revelations 2:10

The devil doesn't believe we can handle the heat. He wants us to give in, but it is just a test. In relationships, yes, we will suffer, but it is just a test. Yes, pain and problems have us in bondage, but it is just for a season. People incarcerated live by a certain code, "Do your time. Don't let your time do you." Be faithful. Be committed, even to the point of death and even to the point it seems like there is no way it could work out. God will give us life as a gift for overcoming the tests. You haven't lived in your relationship until you've overcome some tests together.

Have you ever had a near-death experience? When you realize what you thought was going to take you out didn't, you become a bit more grateful. You feel more alive than you did before the near-death experience. Your perspective on life shifts. Your priorities are realigned. What really matters draws to the forefront of your mind. Foolish thinking is revealed and cast away. We dismiss those small unsettled debts for the desire to unify with those whose lives matter more than the debt, financially or spiritually.

When our relationships face death, and when we survive, the right things are in perspective. We dismiss those small agitations in consideration of just how important we are to one another. Again, in James 1:12 it states "Blessed is the one who perseveres under trial because, having stood the test, that person will receive the crown of life that the Lord has promised to those who love him." And as a reminder, Jesus says that if you love him, you will obey his commandments.

Here's the damaging effect of not enduring or persevering. We lose hope and faith. That's why, even today, people abandon intimacy for pleasure and lust. We trade in love for power. We rage against any covenant with God because we blame him for the lack of happiness and success, which is just as wrong as me blaming my father in the football incident. He'd pick me up from practice and buy me sports drinks to recover. If he was unwilling to sacrifice his time, I wouldn't have even had a chance. I did not make the team because I quit. He never said, "BJ, you can no longer play football." I said that to myself.

Likewise, God never denied us. We denied ourselves because we chose to quit. When we give up on God's way and love, you can imagine the things we would turn to.

The Spirit clearly says that in latter times, some will abandon the faith and follow deceiving spirits and things taught by demons. ~I Timothy 4:1

Keep in mind, this scripture is not speaking of those who rejected the faith. It is referring to those who have abandoned the faith, meaning they once had received it. They once believed and trusted in God, but in later times, after the trials, after outside influences, and after the initial excitement faded away, they had turned away. We receive love so readily at the onset with all of the excitement and new life it brings, but when the work is required, when the trials come, and when the world offers to restore that excitement or rid us of the pain, we abandon love.

What deceiving spirits have you followed? Was it the one that told you you're not good enough? Was it the one that told you you all were just too broken? Was it the one that made you believe that getting into a covenant with God and another soul was a mistake? Was it the one that made your problems seem bigger and more exclusive than they actually were?

What things taught by demons have you followed? To live in your pain and be bitter toward the world? To never forgive when it still hurts? To live for self because you cannot trust anybody? To be promiscuous rather than commit to someone? To curse the ideas of marriage?

And I understand, some of us are really hurting. We experienced so much pain. Believe me, I do sympathize, but there is no healing in holding on to that hurt! We have to let it go. We can overcome it! God has a plan, a path, and a promise for all of us!

Let us not grow weary in well doing, for at the proper time we will reap a harvest if we do not give up.
~Galatians 6:9

This is a very well known scripture. It is a promise from God, and like many of his promises, this is a conditional promise.

Condition number one: We must plant good fruit.
We can't be cold, bitter, arrogant, and selfish. We can't be prideful, unforgiving, lustful, deceiving, and faithless and expect a harvest. These are bad seeds. God will not be mocked by blessing them.

Condition number two: We do not give up!
If we continue to sow good seeds in our relationships, we will see the fruit, eventually. But if we give up, we will not see the fruit.

Notice, God isn't even hanging the promise over your head to tease or torture. We do not have to wait or endure any longer than until the proper time. Continuing to sow seeds breeds discipline, faithfulness, perseverance and trust. If I started reaping too soon, I may stop sowing. If I started reaping too soon, I may entrust too much trust in my own hands than the provision of God. I may overindulge and be a bad steward over the harvest. As much as God is working on our situations, He is also working on us. Your mate's stubbornness is working on your patience. Your mate's insecurities are working on your compassion. You all's problems are constantly working on your faith.

God is purging away all of the impurities. He's breaking off all the useless parts of the wheat. He is making a better you and me. Let's be honest. For some of us, the most we talk to God is only when we have to endure. In the good seasons, we have to remind ourselves to do so, and some of us do it out of a sense of obligation rather than desire. Some of us don't go to church, pray or even read the Bible for ourselves until times are difficult, until nothing else is working, or until we have done all that we can do in our own might. It's at that moment we scream out with all sincerity, "God, have mercy on me!" Then, we return like the prodigal son back to the father.

If you remain in me and my words remain in you, ask whatever you wish, and it will be done for you.
~John 15:7

Love Always Perseveres

Anything we wish for, we could have. Notice that condition, though: if we remain in Him and His word in us. Yet, as I Timothy stated, we abandon our faith so much. We must make it a priority to endure the tests, the trials and the time and remain in faith. The very things that we need and desire in our relationships and in our lives in general would be there. The arguing can go away. The addictions can go away. The hurt can go away. The unforgiveness can go away. The intimacy can be alive and well. The communication can be alive and well. The financial wellness, the dreams and the home can all be there for us, if we endure this season and learn how to both dwell in the Lord and authentically allow Him to dwell in us.

We have to stop complaining about our problems. They will never be the main problem. The fact that our faith is smaller than the trial is the bigger problem. We have to quit whining and whimpering so much. Love is not weak! Our flesh is weak and hopeless. Our spirits understand life is waiting on the other side of the suffering, if we would be strong. Luke 21:19 says "stand firm and you will win life." Life is the reward and prize for enduring. Some of us have yet to live because we check out every time it seems too difficult or too impossible to move forward.

We think we have to climb the mountain, but the Bible says if we would just say to the mountain be removed and cast into the sea, and should believe in our hearts and not doubt, in due season it shall come to pass (Matthew 21:21). Even here, it doesn't promise an immediate response but a certain victory in due season.

I mean, think about it, what if Clark Kent only worked in the office? What if he never functioned as Superman? It would have been a waste of potential. It would have been a waste of power. Love is built for more than just great feelings and happy times. Love is built to endure and to overcome trials, tests and adversities. Love is built to redeem and to conquer! And what good is love if it cannot be used to its potential? Why should we water down what love can do? We need to get to know love better. The things we worry about, love has covered or conquered. The areas we are uncertain about, love has wisdom, discernment and guidance.

And as for [the rest of] you, believers, do not grow tired or lose heart in doing good [but continue doing what is right without weakening]. ~2 Thessalonians 3:13

    Never stop loving. Never stop allowing God's Word to direct you. It gets hard. It seems impossible at times, but God's way is the only promised way. Don't quit. Don't give up. Endure. Persevere. Through the trials, you'll find the path to what you ultimately desire in relationships and in marriage.
    Who will stand the test of time, the trials of life, and the pitfalls of our flesh? Who will reveal the true strength of our spirits? Who will honor God with their hearts? Who will die and rise again with new life? Do not forsake the process. Endure it until the end. Hebrews 6:11 says "we want each of you to show the same diligence to the very end, so that what you hope for may be fully realized." I believe, if you stay in faith, when it is all said and done, you will have known true love. You will have experienced true victory. You will have developed real strength. You will meet the end of your days with joy and peace. You'll leave behind an everlasting legacy of faith. Endure until the end and love will be fully realized. How many times are you going to

start over? You will come back to this degree of testing again and again. There will be a mandatory practice. Are you going to show up or quit?

Therefore, since we are surrounded by such a cloud of witnesses; let us throw off everything that hinders and the sin that so easily entangles. Let us run with perseverance the race marked out for us, fixing our eyes on Jesus, the pioneer and perfector of faith. For the joy set before him he endured the cross, scorning its shame, and sat down at the right hand of God. Consider him who endured such opposition from sinners, so that you will not grow weary and lose heart. ~Hebrews 12:1-3

    During this reconciliation process of ours, there have been so many times I wanted to just research the process of getting a divorce and do it myself. It is not nor has it ever been that I no longer loved my wife or desired to be with her. It can be painful feeling helpless after giving all that you know to give, yet it seems that you are not progressing. It is humiliating to face rejection when you are ready to take that next step in growing closer, yet she is not. It is demeaning to be viewed as the same man from your past, yet you know God has done so much to grow your spirit. Imagine being caught on a string hanging over a cliff. You can't pull yourself up. No one is pulling you up. You feel like you are just dangling there. Suddenly, you are no longer afraid to fall. You just don't want to bear the suspense of wondering if you will be eventually saved.

    I am not asking you to do anything I haven't had to make the hard choice to do. I love my wife. No matter how hard it gets. That will always be true. Moving forward together is always the desire. I am not willing to let pain, fear, insecurity, doubt or temporary division stop me from holding on to what I am believing God will accomplish through us. I've witnessed teams fight through the last seconds of a game and change the outcome from a loss to a victory. I'm playing till the last second.

Let's finish our race. Stop focusing on what deceiving spirits and demons would have us to believe. Yes, the devil will imprison us, but it is only a test. Keep our eyes on Jesus and all of His promises for us. He will never ever lead us astray. Like Jesus, let's set our eyes on the joy of fulfilling our purposes, for obtaining and practicing authentic love. Disregard the shame of the pain; victory is waiting on us. For the sake of love, persevere. Do not grow weary. Do not lose heart.

We Will Get There

I will stand. I will demand a second and third chance before I ever let failure be in the plans.
I'll settle for nothing less than the promised land, cross over the burning sands, just to be forever joined with your hands.
I love you and there's nothing left but to spend the rest of my days demonstrating it in a million ways so that it can never be denied.
With every inch of my being and through every breath that I'm found breathing, I will reveal to you all of my treasures inside.
I'm moving mountains for you.
Understand that, with the power of God, there is nothing I can't do.
And when times get hard my heart will work harder and prove itself stronger and committed until the end.

And when things seem impossible, it will take a lot more to pull me away. Nothing will get in the way of me loving my best friend.

I can't quit. I would never give up. God equips me to live up to the requirements of this relationship.

I can't focus on pain. I'm too involved with purpose. I'm alive inside no matter how it looks on the surface. True love is the final destination. We'll get there the matter how many steps it is.

OUTRO:
Love Never Fails

Love never fails [it never fades nor ends]. But as for prophecies, they will pass away; as for tongues, they will cease; as for the gift of special knowledge, it will pass away. For we know in part, and we prophesy in part [for our knowledge is fragmentary and incomplete]. But when that which is complete and perfect comes, that which is incomplete and partial will pass away. When I was a child, I talked like a child, I thought like a child, I reasoned like a child; when I became a man, I did away with childish things. For now [in this time of imperfection] we see in a mirror dimly [a blurred reflection, a riddle, an enigma], but then [when the time of perfection comes we will see reality] face to face. Now I know in part [just in fragments], but then I will know fully, just as I have been fully known [by God]. And now there remain: faith [abiding trust in God and His promises], hope [confident expectation of eternal salvation], love [unselfish love for others growing out of

God's love for me], these three [the choicest graces]; but the greatest of these is love. ~ I Corinthians 13:8-13 AMP

Love never fades or ends. It doesn't go away. Many will use "lost love" as a reason for divorce, but the reality is that, if love was ever truly there, it still is. We grow cold towards love. We make the choice to stop being directed by love in our actions. Love says forgive. We say no. Love says cover their sin. We say no. The relationship gives way when we decide to give up on love.

As the scripture points out, we are so limited in our understanding and knowledge, even of our own identity. We look in the mirror and see an enigma! We haven't figured ourselves out. I believe as we continue in love, God reveals more of who He has created us to be, but without love, our own identities are never realized. We remain children and never mature into spiritually sound men and women. We refuse to give up our ways of thinking for that of God's ways and commandments. This is why faith is among the things that remain. Only through our faith in God can we can we continue to operate in love and be disciplined in his commands. We will give up, otherwise. We get divorces, otherwise.

With faith and hope, we can come to know ourselves fully as God knows us. We will weather the time to discover that, just as love is, we are more than conquerors! We have to grow up! We have covered a lot of areas of opportunity in ourselves and in our relationships, but be sure to know that we haven't covered everything. I'm sure of that because I admit that I don't know everything to be able to communicate everything to you! Yes, it seems like it is a lot, but I have the faith and hope that God stands behind what He instructs us to do. Through Christ, all of these things are possible!

We have come to know [by personal observation and experience], and have believed [with deep, consistent faith] the love which God has for us. God is love, and the one who abides in love abides in God, and God abides continually in him. In this [union and fellowship with Him], love is completed and perfected with us, so that we may have confidence in the day of judgment [with assurance and boldness to face Him]; because as He is, so are we in the world. ~ I John 4:16-17 AMP

    Notice the importance of the way the connections are arranged in the scripture. It did not say that those who abide in God also abide in love. It said that those who abide in love also abide in God. We cannot choose God without choosing love. Remember the scripture that told us that those who do not know love does not and never has known God. But those of us who will choose love, God chooses to continually abide in us. We become a permanent residency for God, and while he lives in us, it is He who will complete and perfect love with us. We do not accomplish this great feat alone, but we have the most incredible power in the universe working on our behalf, if we believe with deep, consistent faith. Most beautifully, the scripture concludes that we can look at the face of God (a task feared throughout the Bible, especially in the Old Testament) with assurance and boldness because as God, himself is, we were in the world. Those who love as God loves will be actually worthy enough to see His face! The other beautiful part of that is that we can now look in the mirror and see God because we see godliness as it is noted "as He is, so are we in this world." We have the opportunity to be the face of God to our loved ones and this world.

Jesus said to him, "Have I been with you for so long a time, and you do not know Me yet, Philip, nor recognize clearly who I am? Anyone who has seen Me has seen the Father. How can you say, 'Show us the Father?' Do you not believe that I am in the Father, and the Father is in me? The words I say to you I do not say on My own initiative or authority, but the Father, abiding continually in Me, does His works [His attesting miracles and acts of power]. Believe Me that I am in the Father and the Father is in Me; otherwise believe [Me] because of the [very] works themselves [which you have witnessed]. I assure you and most solemnly say to you, anyone who believes in me [as Savior] will also do the things that I do; and he will do even greater things than these [in extent and outreach], because I am going to the Father. And I will do whatever you ask in My name [as My representative], this I will do, so that the Father may be glorified and celebrated in the Son. If you ask Me anything in My name [as My representative], I will do it. "If you [really] love Me, you will keep and obey My commandments. ~ John14:9-15

Not even Christ did things on His own. God abiding continually in Him was the source of His perfection. He goes on to instruct that those who believe in Him could accomplish his examples and more. To love is an access to power. God abides in us and Jesus will do anything we ask him that will bring God glory through his Son. Healthy marriages modeling God's relationship with His church is definitely one of those things that bring Him glory. Bringing up children in a healthy, sound home is definitely another!

I've said several times throughout this book, the character of love is not meant for us to operate in out of our human nature. Christ gives us access to a supernatural force and guide. The Holy Spirit enables us to carry these things out if we will allow ourselves to be directed by Him. Do you trust God enough to follow His directions? Do you truly love Christ? He said, if you did, you would keep and obey His commandments.

We can spend the rest of our lives complaining and being bitter and unhappy about life. We can convince ourselves that we are okay with mediocre relationships. We can whine and whimper and conclude that we are not fit for relationships and true love. However, we can also be convinced that God made us for more. We can walk in faith that perfection is coming, that we will know ourselves as fully as God knows us. We can press through, confidently, knowing that God, our Father abides with us, completing and perfecting love, and Jesus is granting every petition that brings glory to our Heavenly Father.

Let go of the past. Let go of the world's perverted definition of love and relationships. Let go of the natural selfishness we are all born in. Hold on to God's ways and His promises for us. He cares. He has the infinite wisdom to guide us on along the successful path. Your heart is precious. Take good care of it. Pray and ask God to remove the impurities. Humble yourself. Let go of the pride that stands in the way of submitting yourself to God's commandments for love. Your pride isn't protecting you from anything! It only makes our actions foolish before God and the cloud of witnesses. No one, who believes in God, has an excuse for not having successful relationships and marriages. Victory is promised to those who believe. Let God work out our perfect salvation through our experiences, good and bad. Do not give up and do not grow weary. When it is all said and done, you will lack nothing in yourself and in your relationships.

What is love? Love is the most incredible act of God. Love is the most powerful source given to man to influence his actions. Love is the breath of a healthy relationship. Love is the cure to hurt, hate and selfishness. Love is the pathway to peace and joy. Love is the main ingredient to godly character. Love is the personality of the Spirit. Love is a change agent. Love is the strength of a relationship. Love covers. Love conquers.

Reading this book hopefully opened your eyes and your heart, but it is not the end, only the beginning. We have to be willing to walk these things out and become disciplined in love. We must deny our old self daily and constantly rely on the Spirit. Otherwise, we will miss out on the fruit and grow discouraged. Yes, there is grace, but though we rejoice in grace, we must press towards the call. Where grace keeps us from falling, only following God's commands gets us to His promises. Remain in hope. Remain in faith. Trust God enough to do things His way and you will thrive in your relationships. You will overcome all of the opposition: self, the world and Satan!

I searched the Word of God out of a personal hope and plea to understand my role as a husband better and to understand love and marriage. The things He has revealed to me is a great treasure and it is an honor to share them with you. I hope you, too, will take them to heart as I have. If you desire to have a successful love life that honors God in the process, I hope you will pray this prayer with me:

Heavenly Father, thank you for your Word and your instruction. Thank you for your example. I pray your Word will take root in my spirit and correct my heart and guide my life. Lord, I acknowledge the foolishness of my previous understandings and for that reason I will now acknowledge you in all of my ways, especially in matters of the heart. I ask for forgiveness for trusting myself more than I trusted you. From now on, I will operate in absolute faith and trust in you. I, now, trust your ways because I know that your ways are what is best for me and that they lead to the door of all of your promises for me. Let my life and relationship be a light to your people that others, too, will turn to your instruction and Word as a way of living. Father, complete and perfect love in my life and my relationship. Heal all hurts and strengthen our hearts. As I walk in love, I thank you for abiding in me. Let your presence be a source of power and influence in my relationship. I love you, Father. Help me to keep and obey your commandments. In the mighty name of Jesus, I pray. Amen.

May your relationships be fruitful. May God redeem the time and bad experiences. May the power of love restore all of the brokenness and grant peace where there is confusion. May your relationships flourish beyond what you could have ever imagined. May your identity in Christ become clearer and clearer. May you give and experience true, authentic love all the days of your life. Love is not dead, the world is just unfamiliar. May your life and love now serve as an example and a reminder.

Love Strong

Love is not weak. It seeks out the most hurt and heartbroken and restores their souls.
True love is unique. It completes its tasks of reaching out to the lost, lifting them out of ditches and holes.
Love is faithful. God I am so grateful Your love never ran out on me.
Thanks for being an example. Thank you for allowing me to be a sample, imparting that same love to others faithfully.
Love is strong, courageously lifting heavy hearts out of despair and hopelessness.
Love gives new life. Love reaches new heights. Saturate my spirit and my soul so that I may grow in this.
It's time for the world to see Your face. It's time for you to take Your rightful place in our homes and our hearts.
This world has made relationships a disgrace and given marriage a bad taste. Without you, we witness our communities and countries fall apart.
So bear the burden for us again. Strengthen your men and women to come out of themselves to live in a greater glory.
Drown out our natural inclination to sin and feed the spirit within to make choices that brings happy endings to our love story.
We were wrong to ever abandon You. Afterwards we put a burden in a hand or two leaving ourselves weak and discouraged.
Now we're spending time better understanding You. Walking with You intimately is what we plan to do, opening our hearts making them available for Your service.
Love, you are so strong. We were so wrong to ever try to do this thing called life without you.

It's been too long. It's time to return home. We will never again doubt you.

ABOUT THE AUTHOR

BJ O'Neal, Jr. is a devout husband and a proud father. Faced with the decision to either rise from his mistakes or crumble, he is now a pioneer for the well-being of the human spirit, especially in the area of relationships. He wrote and published his first book, *Lovelations - A Journey Through the Ideas of the Mind and Heart.* In this book, he points out the natural conflict involved in the dating process and the pursuit of love. The book promotes a better open-minded perspective of people in order to have a more specific, developed understanding of self so that one can be more intentional with the choices made during the dating process. The goal is to become better and not bitter when disappointment happens. He has sat on many relationship panels throughout his career. He also hosts a segment on a talk show on internet radio, where he discusses matters concerning love and relationships, targeting both the single and married audiences.